SPECTRUM

Test Prep

Grades 1–2

 **Children's Publishing**

Columbus, Ohio

Credits:
McGraw-Hill Children's Publishing Editorial/Art & Design Team
Vincent F. Douglas, *President*
Tracey E. Dils, *Publisher*
Phyllis Sibbing, B.S. Ed., *Project Editor*
Rose Audette, *Art Director*

Also Thanks to:
4ward Communications, Interior Production
Jenny Campbell, Interior Illustration

 **Children's Publishing**

Send all inquiries to:
McGraw-Hill Children's Publishing
8787 Orion Place
Columbus, OH 43240-4027

ISBN 1-57768-662-4

5 6 7 8 9 VHG 07 06 05 04 03

Table of Contents

Just for Parents

About the Tests 4
How to Help Your Child Prepare for Standardized Testing 8

For All Students

Taking Standardized Tests 10
Skills Checklist 12
Getting Ready All Year 20
Homework Log and Weekly Schedule 22
What's Ahead in This Book? 24

Kinds of Questions

Multiple Choice Questions 25
Fill-in-the-Blank Questions 27
Oral Questions 29
Short Answer Questions 31
Choosing a Picture to Answer a Question 33
Math Questions 35
Using a Graph 37
Writing 39

Practice Test and Final Test: Grade 1

Introduction 41
Table of Contents 42
Practice Test 43
Final Test 79
Answer Key 145

Practice Test and Final Test: Grade 2

Introduction 93
Table of Contents 94
Practice Test 95
Final Test 131
Answer Key 147

About the Tests

What Are Standardized Achievement Tests?

Achievement tests measure what children know in particular subject areas such as reading, language arts, and mathematics. They do not measure your child's intelligence or ability to learn.

When tests are standardized, or *normed*, children's test results are compared with those of a specific group who have taken the test, usually at the same age or grade.

Standardized achievement tests measure what children around the country are learning. The test makers survey popular textbook series, as well as state curriculum frameworks and other professional sources, to determine what content is covered widely.

Because of variations in state frameworks and textbook series, as well as grade ranges on some test levels, the tests may cover some material that children have not yet learned. This is especially true if the test is offered early in the school year. However, test scores are compared to those of other children who take the test at the same time of year, so your child will not be at a disadvantage if his or her class has not covered specific material yet.

Different School Districts, Different Tests

There are many flexible options for districts when offering standardized tests. Many school districts choose not to give the full test battery, but select certain content and scoring options. For example, many schools may test only in the areas of reading and mathematics. Similarly, a state or district may use one test for certain grades and another test for other grades. These decisions are often based on

the amount of time and money a district wishes to spend on test administration. Some states choose to develop their own statewide assessment tests.

On pages 6 and 7 you will find information about these five widely used standardized achievement tests:

- California Achievement Test (CAT)
- Terra Nova/CTBS
- Iowa Test of Basic Skills (ITBS)
- Stanford Achievement Test (SAT9)
- Metropolitan Achievement Test (MAT)

However, this book contains strategies and practice questions for use with a variety of tests. Even if your state does not give one of the five tests listed above, your child will benefit from doing the practice questions in this book. If you're unsure about which test your child takes, contact your local school district to find out which tests are given.

Types of Test Questions

Traditionally, standardized achievement tests have used only multiple-choice questions. Today, many tests may include constructed response (short answer) and extended response (essay) questions as well.

In addition, many tests include questions that tap students' higher-order thinking skills. Instead of simple recall questions, such as identifying a date in history, questions may require students to make comparisons and contrasts or analyze results, among other skills.

What the Tests Measure

These tests do not measure your child's level of intelligence, but they do show how well your child knows material that he or she has learned and that is also covered on the tests. It's important to remember that some tests cover content that is not taught in your child's school or grade. In other instances, depending on when in the year the test is given, your child may not yet have covered the material.

If the test reports you receive show that your child needs improvement in one or more skill areas, you may want to seek help from your child's teacher and find out how you can work with your child to improve his or her skills.

California Achievement Test (CAT/5)

What Is the California Achievement Test?

The *California Achievement Test* is a standardized achievement test battery that is widely used with elementary through high school students.

Parts of the Test

The *CAT* includes tests in the following content areas:

Reading
- Word Analysis
- Vocabulary
- Comprehension

Spelling

Language Arts
- Language Mechanics
- Language Usage

Mathematics

Science

Social Studies

Your child may take some or all of these subtests if your district uses the *California Achievement Test*.

Terra Nova/CTBS (Comprehensive Tests of Basic Skills)

What Is the Terra Nova/CTBS?

The *Terra Nova/Comprehensive Tests of Basic Skills* is a standardized achievement test battery used in elementary through high school grades.

While many of the test questions on the *Terra Nova* are in the traditional multiple choice form, your child may take parts of the *Terra Nova* that include some open-ended questions (constructed-response items).

Parts of the Test

Your child may take some or all of the following subtests if your district uses the *Terra Nova/CTBS*:

Reading/Language Arts
Mathematics
Science
Social Studies

Supplementary tests include:
- Word Analysis
- Vocabulary
- Language Mechanics
- Spelling
- Mathematics Computation

Critical thinking skills may also be tested.

Iowa Test of Basic Skills (ITBS)

What Is the ITBS?

The *Iowa Test of Basic Skills* is a standardized achievement test battery used in elementary through high school grades.

Parts of the Test

Your child may take some or all of these subtests if your district uses the *ITBS*, also known as the *Iowa*:

Reading
- Vocabulary
- Reading Comprehension

Language Arts
- Spelling
- Capitalization
- Punctuation
- Usage and Expression

Math
- Concepts/Estimate
- Problems/Data Interpretation

Social Studies

Science

Sources of Information

Stanford Achievement Test (SAT9)

What Is the Stanford Achievement Test?

The *Stanford Achievement Test, Ninth Edition (SAT9)* is a standardized achievement test battery used in elementary through high school grades.

Note that the *Stanford Achievement Test (SAT9)* is a different test from the *SAT* used by high school students for college admissions.

While many of the test questions on the *SAT9* are in traditional multiple choice form, your child may take parts of *the SAT9* that include some open-ended questions (constructed-response items).

Parts of the Test

Your child may take some or all of these subtests if your district uses the *Stanford Achievement Test*:

Reading
- Vocabulary
- Reading Comprehension

Mathematics
- Problem Solving
- Procedures

Language Arts

Spelling

Study Skills

Listening
Critical thinking skills may also be tested.

Metropolitan Achievement Test (MAT7 and MAT8)

What Is the Metropolitan Achievement Test?

The *Metropolitan Achievement Test* is a standardized achievement test battery used in elementary through high school grades.

Parts of the Test

Your child may take some or all of these subtests if your district uses the *Metropolitan Achievement Test*:

Reading
- Vocabulary
- Reading Comprehension

Math
- Concepts and Problem Solving
- Computation

Language Arts
- Pre-writing
- Composing
- Editing

Science

Social Studies

Research Skills

Thinking Skills

Spelling

Statewide Assessments

Today the majority of states give statewide assessments. In some cases these tests are known as *high-stakes assessments*. This means that students must score at a certain level in order to be promoted. Some states use minimum competency or proficiency tests. Often these tests measure more basic skills than other types of statewide assessments.

Statewide assessments are generally linked to state curriculum frameworks. Frameworks provide a blueprint, or outline, to ensure that teachers are covering the same curriculum topics as other teachers in the same grade level in the state. In some states, standardized achievement tests (such as the five described in this book) are used in connection with statewide assessments.

When Statewide Assessments Are Given

Statewide assessments may not be given at every grade level. Generally, they are offered at one or more grades in elementary school, middle school, and high school. Many states test at grades 4, 8, and 10.

State-by-State Information

You can find information about statewide assessments and curriculum frameworks at your state Department of Education Web site. To find the address for your individual state, go to www.ed.gov, click on Topics A–Z, and then click on State Departments of Education. You will find a list of all the state departments of education, mailing addresses, and Web sites.

How to Help Your Child Prepare for Standardized Testing

Preparing All Year Round

Perhaps the most valuable way you can help your child prepare for standardized achievement tests is by providing enriching experiences. Keep in mind also that test results for younger children are not as reliable as for older students. If a child is hungry, tired, or upset, this may result in a poor test score. Here are some tips on how you can help your child do his or her best on standardized tests.

Read aloud with your child. Reading aloud helps develop vocabulary and fosters a positive attitude toward reading. Reading together is one of the most effective ways you can help your child succeed in school.

Share experiences. Baking cookies together, planting a garden, or making a map of your neighborhood are examples of activities that help build skills that are measured on the tests, such as sequencing and following directions.

Become informed about your state's testing procedures. Ask about or watch for announcements of meetings that explain about standardized tests and statewide assessments in your school district. Talk to your child's teacher about your child's individual performance on these state tests during a parent-teacher conference.

Help your child know what to expect. Read and discuss with your child the test-taking tips in this book. Your child can prepare by working through a couple of strategies a day so that no practice session takes too long.

Help your child with his or her regular school assignments. Set up a quiet study area for homework. Supply this area with pencils, paper, markers, a calculator, a ruler, a dictionary, scissors, glue, and so on. Check your child's homework and offer to help if he or she gets stuck. But remember, it's your child's homework, not yours. If you help too much, your child will not benefit from the activity.

Keep in regular contact with your child's teacher. Attend parent-teacher conferences, school functions, PTA or PTO meetings, and school board meetings. This will help you get to know the educators in your district and the families of your child's classmates.

Learn to use computers as an educational resource. If you do not have a computer and Internet access at home, try your local library.

Remember—simply getting your child comfortable with testing procedures and helping him or her know what to expect can improve test scores!

Getting Ready for the Big Day

There are lots of things you can do on or immediately before test day to improve your child's chances of testing success. What's more, these strategies will help your child prepare him- or herself for school tests, too, and promote general study skills that can last a lifetime.

Provide a good breakfast on test day.
Instead of sugar cereal, which provides immediate but not long-term energy, have your child eat a breakfast with protein or complex carbohydrates, such as an egg, whole grain cereal or toast, or a banana-yogurt shake.

Promote a good night's sleep. A good night's sleep before the test is essential. Try not to overstress the importance of the test. This may cause your child to lose sleep because of anxiety. Doing some exercise after school and having a quiet evening routine will help your child sleep well the night before the test.

Assure your child that he or she is not expected to know all of the answers on the test. Explain that other children in higher grades may take the same test, and that the test may measure things your child has not yet learned in school. Help your child understand that you expect him or her to put forth a good effort—and that this is enough. Your child should not try to cram for these tests. Also avoid threats or bribes; these put undue pressure on children and may interfere with their best performance.

Keep the mood light and offer encouragement. To provide a break on test days, do something fun and special after school—take a walk around the neighborhood, play a game, read a favorite book, or prepare a special snack together. These activities keep your child's mood light—even if the testing sessions have been difficult—and show how much you appreciate your child's effort.

Taking Standardized Tests

What You Need to Know About Taking Tests

You can get better at taking tests. Here are some tips.

Do your schoolwork. Study in school. Do your homework all the time. These things will help you in school and on any tests you take. Learn new things a little at a time. Then you will remember them better when you see them on a test.

Feel your best. One way you can do your best on tests and in school is to make sure your body is ready. Get a good night's sleep. Eat a healthy breakfast.

One more thing: Wear comfortable clothes. You can also wear your lucky shirt or your favorite color on test day. It can't hurt. It may even make you feel better about the test.

Be ready for the test. Do practice questions. Learn about the different kinds of questions. Books like this one will help you.

Follow the test directions. Listen carefully to the directions your teacher gives. Read all instructions carefully. Watch out for words such as *not*, *none, never*, *all*, and *always*. These words can change the meaning of the directions. You may want to circle words like these. This will help you keep them in mind as you answer the questions.

Look carefully at each page before you start. Do reading tests in a special order. First, read the directions. Read the questions next. This way you will know what to look for as you read. Then read the story. Last, read the story again quickly. Skim it to find the best answer.

On math tests, look at the labels on graphs and charts. Think about what the graph or chart shows. You will often need to draw conclusions about the information to answer some questions.

Use your time wisely. Many tests have time limits. Look at the clock when the test starts. Figure out when you need to stop. When you begin, look over the whole thing. Do the easy parts first. Go back and do the hard parts last. Make sure you do not spend too much time on any one part. This way, if you run out of time, you still have completed much of the test.

Fill in the answer circles the right way. Fill in the whole circle. Make your pencil mark dark, but not so dark that it goes through the paper! Be sure you pick just one answer for each question. If you pick two answers, both will be marked as wrong.

Use context clues to figure out hard questions. You may come across a word or an idea you don't understand. First, try to say it in your own words. Then use context clues— the words in the sentences nearby— to help you figure out its meaning.

Sometimes it's good to guess. Here's what to do. Each question may have four or five answer choices. You may know that two answers are wrong, but you are not sure about the rest. Then make your best guess. If you are not sure about any of the answers, skip it. Do not guess. Tests like these take away extra points for wrong answers. So it is better to leave them blank.

Check your work. You may finish the test before the time is up. Then you can go back and check your answers. Make sure you answered each question you could. Also, make sure that you filled in only one answer circle for each question. Erase any extra marks on the page.

Finally—stay calm! Take time to relax before the test. One good way to relax is to get some exercise. Stretch, shake out your fingers, and wiggle your toes. Take a few slow, deep breaths. Then picture yourself doing a great job!

Skills Checklists

In which subjects do you need more practice? Find out. Use the checklists for your grade. Read each sentence. Is it true for you? Put a check next to it. Then look at the unchecked sentences. These are the skills you need to review.

Keep in mind that if you are using these checklists in the middle of the school year, you may not have learned some skills yet. Talk to your teacher or a parent if you need help with a new skill.

Reading, Language Arts, and Writing: Grade 1

Reading

- ❑ I can find the main idea.
- ❑ I can note details.
- ❑ I can understand characters' feelings.
- ❑ I can figure out the author's purpose for writing.
- ❑ I use information from a story and what I already know to make inferences and draw conclusions.
- ❑ I can compare and contrast.
- ❑ I can find what happens first, next, and last.
- ❑ I can predict what will happen next in a story.
- ❑ I can choose the best title for a story.

Language Arts

I can identify and use different parts of speech.

- ❑ nouns or naming words
- ❑ plurals or nouns that name more than one
- ❑ verbs or action words
- ❑ adjectives or describing words
- ❑ pronouns

- ❑ I can tell the difference between a complete and an incomplete sentence.
- ❑ I can change a telling sentence to an asking sentence.
- ❑ I use end punctuation correctly.
- ❑ I use capital letters correctly.

Writing

Before I write

❏ I think about who will read my work.

❏ I think about my purpose for writing (to inform or entertain).

When I write a draft

❏ It has a main idea and supporting details.

❏ I use words and actions that tell about my characters.

❏ I use words that tell about the setting.

As I revise my work

❏ I check for spelling, capitalization, punctuation, and grammar mistakes.

❏ I take out parts that are not necessary.

❏ I add words and sentences to make my work more interesting.

❏ I neatly write or type my final copy.

❏ I include my name and a title on the finished work.

Word Analysis/Phonics

❏ I can find root words.

❏ I understand prefixes and suffixes.

I can match

❏ beginning sounds

❏ ending sounds

❏ vowel sounds

Vocabulary

❏ I can use context clues to figure out hard words.

❏ I know what synonyms are.

❏ I can find words with opposite meanings.

❏ I can read sight words.

❏ I can find written words from spoken definitions.

Mathematics: Grade 1

Numeration

- ☐ I can count to 100.

- ☐ I can count objects to 100.

- ☐ I can compare groups of objects.

- ☐ I can read numbers from 0 to 100.

- ☐ I can count on by 2s, 3s, 4s, 5s, and 10s.

- ☐ I can find the ones place and the tens place in a number and tell what that means.

Addition and Subtraction

- ☐ I know addition and subtraction facts to 18.

- ☐ I can add two-digit numbers with no regrouping.

- ☐ I write and solve number sentences.

Problem Solving

❑ When I do number problems, I read the directions carefully.

❑ When I do word problems, I read the problem carefully.

❑ I look for words that tell whether I must add or subtract to solve the problem.

Time, Measurement, Money, and Geometry

❑ I can use charts and graphs.

❑ I can tell time on both kinds of clocks.

❑ I can measure lengths.

❑ I understand how much coins are worth.

❑ I know the basic shapes.

❑ I can match shape patterns.

❑ I can find lines of symmetry.

Reading, Language Arts, and Writing: Grade 2

Reading

- ☐ I can find the main idea.
- ☐ I can note details.
- ☐ I can understand characters' feelings.
- ☐ I can figure out the author's purpose for writing.
- ☐ I use information from a story and what I already know to make inferences and draw conclusions.
- ☐ I understand similes.
- ☐ I can compare and contrast.
- ☐ I can find what happens first, next, and last.
- ☐ I can predict what will happen next in a story.
- ☐ I can choose the best title for a story.

Language Arts

- ☐ I can identify and use the different parts of speech
- ☐ common and proper nouns
- ☐ plural nouns
- ☐ pronouns
- ☐ verbs
- ☐ adjectives
- ☐ I can tell the difference between a complete sentence and an incomplete sentence.
- ☐ I can tell the difference between a correctly written sentence and an incorrectly written one.
- ☐ I use end punctuation correctly.
- ☐ I use capital letters correctly.
- ☐ I can tell the difference between a correctly spelled word and an incorrectly spelled one.

Writing

Before I write

☐ I think about who will read my work.

☐ I think about my purpose for writing (to inform or entertain).

When I write a draft

☐ It has a main idea and supporting details.

☐ I use words and actions that tell about my characters.

☐ I use words that tell about the setting.

As I revise my work

☐ I check for spelling, capitalization, punctuation, and grammar mistakes.

☐ I take out parts that are not necessary.

☐ I add words and sentences to make my work more interesting.

☐ I neatly write or type my final copy.

☐ I include my name and a title on the finished work.

Word Analysis/Phonics

☐ I can find root words.

☐ I understand prefixes and suffixes.

I can match

☐ beginning sounds

☐ ending sounds

☐ vowel sounds

Vocabulary

☐ I can use context clues to figure out hard words.

☐ I know what synonyms are.

☐ I can find antonyms.

☐ I can find compound words.

☐ I can define words that have more than one meaning.

☐ I can form contractions for words.

Mathematics: Grade 2

Numeration

- ☐ I can read numbers to 1000.

- ☐ I can count objects to 1000.

- ☐ I can compare numbers.

- ☐ I can count on by 2s, 3s, 4s, 5s, and 10s.

- ☐ I understand place value to the hundreds place.

- ☐ I can put numbers in order.

- ☐ I can complete number patterns.

Addition, Subtraction, and Multiplication

- ☐ I know addition and subtraction facts to 18.

- ☐ I can add and subtract two- and three-digit numbers with regrouping.

- ☐ I can multiply one-digit numbers by 2, 3, 4, 5, and 10.

- ☐ I can write and solve number sentences.

Problem Solving

- ☐ When I do number problems, I read the directions carefully.

- ☐ When I do word problems, I read the problem carefully.

- ☐ I look for words that tell whether I must add or subtract to solve the problem.

Time, Measurement, Money, and Geometry

- ☐ I can use charts and graphs.

- ☐ I can understand a calendar.

- ☐ I can tell time on both kinds of clocks.

- ☐ I can use basic measuring tools.

- ☐ I can compare and measure lengths.

- ☐ I understand how much coins are worth.

- ☐ I know the basic shapes.

- ☐ I can match and complete shape patterns.

- ☐ I can find lines of symmetry.

- ☐ I understand basic fractions.

Getting Ready All Year

You can do better in school and on tests if you know how to study and make good use of your time. Here are some tips.

Make it easy to get your homework done. Set up a place in which to do it each day. Choose a place that is quiet. Get the things you need, such as pencils, paper, and markers. Put them in your homework place.

Homework Log and Weekly Calendar Make your own homework log. Or copy the one on pages 22–23 of this book. Write down your homework each day. Also list other things you have to do, such as sports practice or music lessons. Then you won't forget easily.

Do your homework right away. Do it soon after you get home from school. Give yourself a lot of time. Then you won't be too tired to do it later on.

Get help if you need it. If you need help, just ask. Call a friend. Or ask a family member. If they cannot help you, ask your teacher the next day.

Figure out how you learn best. Some people learn best by listening, others by looking. Some learn best by doing something with their hands or moving around. Some children like to work in groups. And some are very happy working alone.

Think about your favorite parts of school. Are you good in art, mathematics, or maybe gym? Your favorite class maybe a clue to how you learn best. Try to figure it out. Then use it to study and learn better.

Practice, practice, practice! The best way to get better is by practicing a lot. You may have trouble in a school subject. Do some extra work in that subject. It can give you just the boost you need.

Homework Log
and Weekly Schedule

	MONDAY	TUESDAY	WEDNESDAY
MATHEMATICS			
READING			
LANGUAGE ARTS			
OTHER			

for the week of _____

THURSDAY	FRIDAY	SATURDAY/SUNDAY	
			MATHEMATICS
			READING
			LANGUAGE ARTS
			OTHER

What's Ahead in This Book?

Everyone in school has to take tests. This book will help you get ready for them. Ask a family member to help you.

The best way to get ready for tests is to do your best in school. You can also learn about the kinds of questions that will be on them. That is what this book is about. It will help you know what to do on the day of the test.

You will learn about the questions that will be on the test. You will get questions on which to practice. You will get hints for how to answer the questions.

In the last part of this book, there is a Practice Test and Final Test for Grade 1 and a Practice Test and Final Test for Grade 2. These tests look like the ones you take in school. There is also a list of answers to help you check your answers.

If you practice, you will be all ready on test day.

Multiple Choice Questions

A multiple choice question has 3 or 4 answer choices.
You must choose the right answer.

EXAMPLE   **Which word does *not* fit in this group?**

dog, cat, _____

○ hamster

○ goldfish

○ bike

Sometimes you will know the answer right away. Other times you won't. To answer multiple choice questions on a test, do the following:

• Always read or listen to the directions.

• Look at each answer first. Then mark which one you think is right.

• Answer easy questions first.

• Skip hard questions. Come back to them later. Circle the question to remember which ones you still need to do.

Testing It Out
Now look at the sample question more closely.

Think: Dogs and cats are both pets. I see the word *not*. I need a word that is not a kind of pet. Hamsters and goldfish are pets. I know that a bike is not a pet. I will choose bike.

Multiple Choice Practice

Directions: Find the word that means the same thing, or almost the same thing, as the underlined word. Fill in the circle next to your answer.

Directions: Find the word that rhymes with the underlined word. Fill in the circle next to your answer.

1 <u>delicious</u> pizza

○ boring

○ hungry

○ tasty

3 I am afraid of <u>mice</u>.

○ bears

○ rice

○ moose

2 <u>below</u> the desk

○ above

○ behind

○ under

4 I like to eat spaghetti <u>dinner</u>.

○ winner

○ supper

○ finger

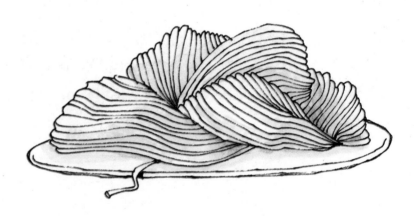

Fill-in-the-Blank Questions

On some tests you must find a word that is missing from a sentence.

EXAMPLE _____ **your teeth before you go to bed.**

- ○ Smile

- ○ Brush

- ○ Buy

To answer fill-in-the-blank questions:

- Try to think of the answer before you look at the choices.

- See if one of the choices matches your answer.

- Always check the other choices. There may be a better answer.

Testing It Out

Now look at the sample question above more closely.

 **Think:** *Smile* reminds me of teeth. But it does not make sense. *Brush* seems right. I will look at all the choices. *Buy* starts with the same letter as *Brush*. But it does not make sense. I will mark *Brush*.

Fill-in-the-Blank Practice

Directions: Find the word that best completes the sentence. Fill in the circle next to your answer.

1 **The cereal is _____.**

○ in the bowl

○ at a movie

○ in the attic

2 **The _____ is full of apples.**

○ tall tree

○ blue sea

○ big building

3 **When I am thirsty, I _____.**

○ chop wood

○ sing songs

○ drink water

4 **We had cake at my birthday _____.**

○ hike

○ party

○ flower

5 **Be _____ not to touch the oven.**

○ careful

○ happy

○ silly

Oral Questions

On some tests you will listen to your teacher read a word. Then you will answer a question about the sounds. Ask an adult to read you the questions.

EXAMPLE **Which word starts with the same sound as *dish*?**

○ plate

○ door

○ bath

To answer oral questions:

• Listen to the directions.

• Say each answer to yourself. Listen to the sounds.

• Look at all the words. Then mark the one you think is correct.

Testing It Out

Now look at the sample question more closely.

Think: *Plate* means the same thing as *dish*. But it does not start with the same sound. *Door* starts with the same sound as *dish*. *Bath* does not start with the same sound. *Door* must be the right answer.

Oral Questions Practice

Directions: Listen to an adult say the word.
Fill in the circle next to the word that starts with same sound.

1 desk

   ○ chair   ○ bat   ○ den

Directions: Listen to an adult say the word. Fill in the circle next to the word that ends with same sound.

2 make

   ○ man   ○ nose   ○ rock

Directions: Listen to an adult say the word. Fill in the circle next to the word that rhymes.

3 find

   ○ left   ○ fun   ○ kind

Short Answer Questions

Some questions do not give you answers to choose from.
You must write short answers in your own words.

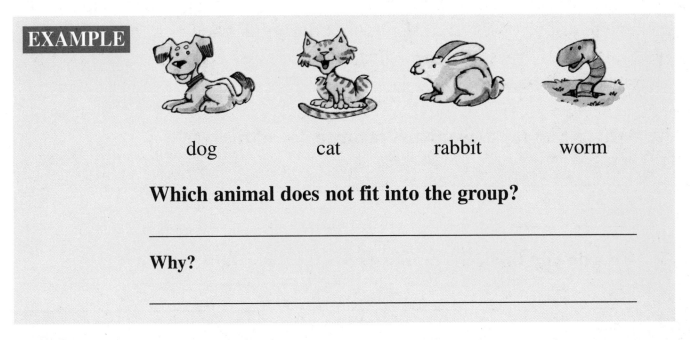

EXAMPLE

dog   cat   rabbit   worm

Which animal does not fit into the group?

_____

Why?

_____

When you write short answers to questions on a test:

- Read each question. Make sure you answer the question. Do not write other things about the words or pictures.

- Your answer should be short. But make sure you answer the whole question.

- Write complete sentences.

Testing It Out

Now look at the sample question more closely.

Think: Dogs, cats, and rabbits have four legs and fur. But worms do not have legs or fur. So *worm* is the answer.

Which animal does not fit into the group?
The worm does not fit into the group.

Why?
The other animals have four legs and fur. A worm does not.

Short Answer Practice

Directions: Read the story. Then answer the questions.

Every Sunday I go with my dad to play basketball in the park. He teaches me how to dribble, pass, even slam-dunk! Sometimes he has to lift me up to reach the net. He says I will be a great player when I get taller. Sunday is my favorite day of the week.

1 **Why is Sunday the author's favorite day of the week?**

_____

_____

2 **How do you think the author feels about her father? Why?**

_____

_____

Directions: Look at the pictures to decide which one does not belong. Write your answers on the lines.

3

cup   plate   book

Which picture does not belong?

_____

Why?

_____

Choosing a Picture to Answer a Question

Sometimes your teacher will read you a story and ask you a question about it. You will choose the picture that best answers the question. Ask an adult to read this story to you.

EXAMPLE Carly and Mike were best friends. One day they were playing hide and seek in Mike's back yard. Carly could not find Mike anywhere. Carly gave up and went into their tree house. She was very surprised when Mike popped out and said "boo!"

Where was Mike hiding?

○   ○   ○

When you choose a picture to answer a question on a test:

• Listen to the story carefully.

• Try to imagine what is happening. Choose the picture that is closest to what you imagine.

• Mark your answer as soon as you know which one is right. Then get ready for the next question.

• Change your answer only if you are sure it is wrong and another one is right.

Testing It Out

Now look at the sample question more closely. Where was Mike hiding?

 **Think:** Mike did not hide *behind* a tree in the story. He did not hide *under* a bed. They were playing in the back yard. Mike was hiding in a tree house. The third picture is right.

Choosing a Picture
to Answer a Question Practice

Directions: Listen to the story. Then choose the picture that best answers the question.

Wendy was Tanya's baby sister. Wendy wanted to do everything Tanya did. Tanya was going to eat the last piece of cake. Wendy wanted a piece too. Tanya got an idea. She cut the piece of cake in half. They ate their snack together.

1   Which picture shows Wendy?

○   ○   ○

2   What did Wendy want to eat?

○   ○   ○

Math Questions

On some tests, you will have to answer math questions. Some of these questions will tell a story or show pictures.

EXAMPLE

Look at the picture. Which number sentence shows how many treats there are in all?

○   1 + 2 + 1

○   4 + 6

○   3 + 2 + 1

When you answer math questions on a test:

• Look at the picture. Read all the choices. Then mark your answer.

• Look for important words and numbers.

• Draw pictures or write numbers on scratch paper.

• Look for clue words like *in all, more, less, left,* and *equal.*

Testing It Out

Look at the sample question more closely.

 **Think:** I see 3 groups of treats. The number sentence should have 3 numbers. The first sentence has 3 numbers. But it does not match the pictures. The next sentence only has 2 numbers. They are also too big. The last sentence matches the picture. There are 3 cookies, 2 lollipops, and 1 candy bar.

Math Questions Practice

Directions: Fill in the circle next to the answer that matches the picture.

1

- ○ 39 cents
- ○ 40 cents
- ○ 50 cents

2

- ○ 13 books
- ○ 11 books
- ○ 14 books

Directions: Use scratch paper to work out your answer.
Then fill in the circle next to the right number.

3

$$\begin{array}{r} 26 \\ + 7 \\ \hline \end{array}$$

- ○ 33
- ○ 36
- ○ 39

4

$$\begin{array}{r} 11 \\ 21 \\ + 32 \\ \hline \end{array}$$

- ○ 34
- ○ 54
- ○ 64

Using a Graph

You will have to read a graph to answer some questions.

EXAMPLE

Who read the same amount of books?

○   Barbara and Tom

○   Sue and Barbara

○   Sammy and Sue

When answering graph questions:

• Read the question carefully.

• Look for clue words such as *most*, *least*, *same*, *more*, and *less*.

• You don't always need to count. Try to see how much of each column or row is filled in.

Testing It Out
Now look at the sample question more closely.

Think: Barbara read 2 books and Tom only read 1. Sue read 2 books and Barbara read 2 books. That is the same number. Sammy read 3 books and Sue read 2. The answer is Sue and Barbara.

Using a Graph Practice

Directions: The graph shows how many children get to school by bus, car, train, bike, and walking. Look at the graph. Then fill in the circle next to your answer.

1 How do most children get to school?

○ Bus

○ Car

○ Train

○ Bike

○ Walk

2 How many children walk to school?

○ 10

○ 15

○ 20

3 Do more children ride in cars or on the train?

○ Car

○ Train

Writing

On some tests you will have to write a long answer to a question. The question is called a writing prompt. Sometimes you may have to write a paragraph or a story.

| EXAMPLE | **Think of one thing that you do outside that you enjoy. Tell what you enjoy doing outside and why.** |

When answering writing prompts:

- Write about something you know.

- Read the prompt carefully. Answer every part of the question.

- Plan your time. Leave enough time to check for spelling, punctuation, and grammar mistakes when you are finished.

Testing It Out

Look at the sample prompt more closely.

Think: I want to write about something I really like to do. Let's see, what is my favorite thing to do? I like to play drums. But I do not do that outside. What is my favorite thing to do outside? I love to climb trees. I am a very good climber.

When I am outside, I like to climb trees. I know how to climb every tree in my backyard. I like climbing trees because when I get to the top, I can see down our whole street. Sometimes I see my friends and wave to them. Sometimes I feel like a bird looking down from the sky. Climbing trees makes me happy.

Writing Practice

Directions: Think of one thing you want to learn to do. What is it? Why do you want to learn how to do it? How can you learn it? Write your answers on the lines.

_____

_____

_____

_____

_____

_____

_____

_____

_____

_____

_____

_____

_____

_____

Grade 1 Introduction to Practice Test and Final Test

On page 43, you will find Grade 1 Practice Test. On page 79, you will find Grade 1 Final Test. These tests will give you a chance to put the tips you have learned to work.

Here are some things to remember as you take these tests:

- Read and listen carefully to all the directions.

- Be sure you understand all the directions before you begin.

- Ask an adult questions about the directions if you do not understand them.

- Work as quickly as you can during each test.

- Using a pencil, make sure to fill in only one little answer circle for each question. Don't mark outside the circle. If you change an answer, be sure to erase your first mark completely.

- If you're not sure about an answer, you can guess.

- Use the tips you have learned whenever you can.

- It is OK to be a little nervous. You may even do better.

- When you complete all the lessons in this book, you will be on your way to test success!

Grade 1 Table of Contents

Practice Test

Unit 1: Reading and Language Arts

Lesson 1: Story Reading 43
Lesson 2: Reading a Poem 50
Lesson 3: Writing 54
Lesson 4: Review 56

Unit 2: Basic Skills

Lesson 1: Word Analysis 60
Lesson 2: Vocabulary 63
Lesson 3: Computation 66
Lesson 4: Review 67

Unit 3: Mathematics

Lesson 1: Mathematics Skills 71
Lesson 2: Review 76

Final Test

Unit 1: Reading and Language Arts 79

Unit 2: Basic Skills 85

Unit 3: Mathematics 89

Answer Key 146

Reading and Language Arts

Lesson 1 **Story Reading**

Directions: Find the words that fit best.

SAMPLE A

The toast is _____.

on the dish   playing ball   in the closet

○   ○   ○   .

Directions: Listen to the story: Jonathan Harrison Turtle was in quite a fix. He had been taking his daily walk, when suddenly an owl had flown down and landed on his head.

SAMPLE B

Which picture shows what happened to the turtle?

The turtle met
a rabbit.

The turtle was
on the owl.

The owl was
on the turtle.

○   ○   ○

Listen carefully to the directions.

Think about what you are supposed to do.

Look at each answer before marking the one you think is right.

GO

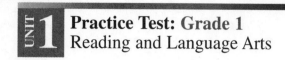
Directions: Listen to the story: Carol wanted to ride her bike with her friend, Ramon. They would ride up the street to the playground. When she went to get her bike, Carol saw it had a flat tire.

1   **Which picture shows what was wrong with Carol's bike?**

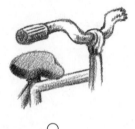      

○   ○   ○

2   **Find the picture that shows where Ramon and Carol wanted to go.**

○   ○   ○

3   **Find the sentence that tells how Carol probably felt when she saw her bike.**

She was happy.   She was sad.   She didn't care.

○   ○   ○

Listen to the rest of the story: Carol told her big brother about the tire. He said he could fix it right away. He fixed the tire, and Carol could ride with her friend.

4   **Mark the circle under the words that tell what this story was mostly about.**

going for a ride   fixing a bike   going to the playground

○   ○   ○

GO

Directions: Find the word that has the same beginning sound as <u>street</u>.

5   strong   teeth   horse

       ○   ○   ○

Directions: Find the word that has the same beginning sound as <u>flat</u>.

6   tall   sat   fly

       ○   ○   ○

Directions: Find the word that has the same middle sound as <u>ride</u>.

7   miss   line   hair

       ○   ○   ○

Directions: Find the word that has the same middle sound as <u>get</u>.

8   ten   here   real

       ○   ○   ○

GO

Directions: Many people in every neighborhood have pets. This story is about a boy and his pet. Read the story, then do numbers 9–12.

My dog's name is Nick. He is big and has long, brown hair. He likes to chase a ball. If I throw a ball, he catches it in his mouth. Brings it back to me. When I'm at school, Nick waits for me. He is standing near the door when I get home. He jumps up and licks my face. Then we go outside for a walk.

Francisco

GO

9 **What does Nick look like?**

He has long,   He is white   He is small with
brown hair.   with spots.   curly hair.

○   ○   ○

---

10 **Where is Nick when Francisco gets home?**

○   in the kitchen

○   on the bed

○   by the door

---

11 **If Francisco throws a stick, Nick will probably**

○   catch a ball.

○   bring it back.

○   lick his face.

GO

12   **Which of these is the best name for the story?**

○   My Dog Nick

○   Chasing a Ball

○   Walking the Dog

---

13   **This is Nick's ball.**

○   Is this Nick's ball?

○   Nick's ball is this?

○   Ball is this Nick's

---

14   **Brings it back to me is not a complete sentence. What should Francisco add to make it a complete sentence?**

_____ **brings it back to me.**

○   They

○   I

○   He

GO

15 **I take care of the dog.**
I walk the dog.

_____ .

I go to school.

I wash the dog.

I read a book.

---

16 **I am having a snack.**
I eat an apple.

_____ .

Mother is at work.

I like to go swimming.

Then I drink some milk.

STOP

Lesson 2 Reading a Poem

Directions: Listen to the poem. The kitten curled up on my lap.
Pretty soon, it took a nap.

SAMPLE A

Which picture shows who took a nap?

○ ○ ○

SAMPLE B

Which word has the same beginning sound as <u>pull</u>?

pick   drip   desk

○ ○ ○

Think about the poem while you listen to it.

Mark your answer as soon as you know which one is right.

Change your answer only if you are sure
it is wrong.

GO

Directions: Listen to the poem. In the same house whose color is blue
Are lots of toy animals in Marilyn's zoo.

1   **Find the picture that shows where the zoo is.**

○   ○   ○

2   **Find the picture that shows which might be in the zoo.**

○   ○   ○

Listen to the next part of the poem.
Some are small like Reggie Raccoon,
But others are huge, like Betty Baboon.

3   **Find the picture that shows what Reggie is.**

○   ○   ○

GO

4 **Which picture shows Marilyn with Betty Baboon?**

   ○   ○   ○

Listen to the last part of the poem: Marilyn's bedroom is home to the zoo,
If you ever visit, she'll show it to you.

5 **Find the picture that shows where Marilyn keeps her animals.**

   ○   ○   ○

6 **Find the picture that shows what Marilyn would want to do first if someone visited her.**

   ○   ○   ○

GO

Directions: Find the word that has the same beginning sound as <u>large</u>.

7

        leaf   arm   hill
         ○   ○   ○

Directions: Find the word that has the same beginning sound as <u>golf</u>.

8

        fox   tall   gone
        ○   ○   ○

Directions: Find the word that has the same middle sound as <u>hat</u>.

9

    bag   buy   bit

     ○   ○   ○

Directions: Find the word that has the same middle sound as <u>wet</u>.

10

    room   rest   roll

     ○   ○   ○

STOP

Lesson 3 Writing

Directions: Read the paragraph of information.

Cats are mammals. They have soft fur and long tails. Many cats live with people. These cats eat cat food. Wild cats may eat birds, bugs, or garbage. Cats meow when they are hungry. They purr when they are happy.

Directions: Think of an animal. Write a paragraph about it. Answer these questions:

- **How does the animal look?**

- **Where does it live?**

- **What does it eat?**

- **What are some of the things it does?**

GO

Directions: Read the sentences that tell how to feed a hamster.

How to Feed a Hamster

Step 1. Get one scoop of food.

Step 2. Open the hamster's cage.

Step 3. Fill its bowl with food.

Step 4. Close the cage.

Directions: Think of something you can do or make. Write how-to sentences on the numbered lines below.

How to _____

Step 1 _____

_____

Step 2 _____

_____

Step 3 _____

_____

Step 4 _____

_____

STOP

Lesson 4 Review

Directions: Find the word that has the same beginning sound as <u>easy</u>.

   end   eat   ask

   ○   ○   ○

Directions: Find the word that has the same middle sound as <u>book</u>.

1   face   foot   find

    ○   ○   ○

2   The toy is on the bed.

    ○   ○   ○

3   The door is open.

    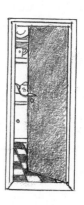

    ○   ○   ○

GO

Directions: Listen to the story. Steven and his little sister were playing in the yard. They saw a bird land on the fence beside the house.

4   Who was with Steven?

○   ○   ○

5   Where did the bird land?

○   ○   ○

6   Where were they playing?

They were in the yard.	They were in school.	They were on the steps.
○	○	○

Directions: Listen to the story. The bird flew to the ground and picked up some dead grass. Then it flew into a tree. Steven said that the bird was building a nest.

7   What is the story mostly about?

two friends   playing a game   what a bird did
○   ○   ○

GO

Directions: For numbers 8 and 9, choose the correct end mark.

8 Dear Grandmother _____

.   ,   ?
○   ○   ○

9 Thank you for the gift _____

?   ,   .
○   ○   ○

Directions: For numbers 10 and 11, mark the part of the sentence that needs a capital letter.

10   the coat | keeps me | very warm.
        ○   ○   ○

11   With | much love, | chris
        ○   ○   ○

GO

Directions: Read the paragraph that describes a special day.

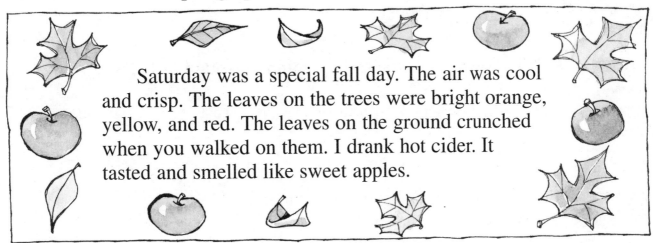

Saturday was a special fall day. The air was cool and crisp. The leaves on the trees were bright orange, yellow, and red. The leaves on the ground crunched when you walked on them. I drank hot cider. It tasted and smelled like sweet apples.

Directions: Think about a special day. Write words in the web that describe your day.

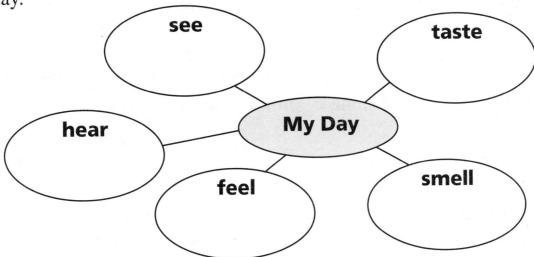

Directions: Write a paragraph that describes your special day. Use the ideas in your web.

_____

_____

_____

_____

STOP

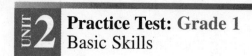
Basic Skills

Lesson 1 Word Analysis

Directions: Which word has the same beginning sound as <u>bell</u>?

SAMPLE A

hill ○   boat ○   rest ○   cab ○

TIPS Say each answer to yourself.
Listen for the beginning sound.

1 Which word has the same beginning sound as <u>new</u>?

when ○   tent ○   neat ○   shoe ○

2 Which word has the same beginning sound as <u>dark</u>?

desk ○   park ○   sad ○   warm ○

3 Which word has the same beginning sound as <u>friend</u>?

cry ○   trip ○   from ○

4 Which word has the same beginning sound as <u>play</u>?

please ○   stay ○   chain ○

5 Which word has the same beginning sound as <u>skin</u>?

clown ○   skip ○   slow ○

GO

Directions: Which word has the same ending sound as <u>far</u>?

SAMPLE
B

fun   off   ran   her
○   ○   ○   ○

TIPS   Say each answer to yourself.
Listen for the ending sound.

6   **Which word has the same ending sound as <u>pin</u>?**

trap   can   nose   pet
○   ○   ○   ○

7   **Which word has the same ending sound as <u>hit</u>?**

not   hear   win   dish
○   ○   ○   ○

8   **Which word has the same ending sound as <u>have</u>?**

wish   head   van   love
○   ○   ○   ○

9   **Which word has the same ending sound as <u>want</u>?**

wind   sent   both
○   ○   ○

10   **Which word has the same ending sound as <u>dirt</u>?**

learn   bird   heart
○   ○   ○

GO

Directions: Which word has the same middle sound as <u>cup</u>?

SAMPLE C

turn ○   must ○   shout ○   hurt ○

TIPS   Say each answer to yourself.
Listen for the middle sound.

11   Which word has the same middle sound as <u>peach</u>?

quiet ○   push ○   last ○   need ○

12   Which word has the same middle sound as <u>plane</u>?

cake ○   rag ○   pants ○   mark ○

13   Which word has the same middle sound as <u>block</u>?

voice ○   should ○   sock ○   roof ○

14   Which word has the same beginning sound as <u>eagle</u>?

ant ○   and ○   end ○   eat ○

STOP

Lesson 2 Vocabulary

Directions: Find the word that means <u>big</u>.

SAMPLE A

funny ○   cool ○   large ○   empty ○

TIPS

Think about the definition.
Choose the best answer.

1 **Find the word that means twelve months.**

yard ○   year ○   pail ○   mile ○

2 **Find the word that means a kind of fruit.**

tree ○   bread ○   milk ○   orange ○

3 **Find the word that means a place where people live.**

house ○   chair ○   roof ○   tree ○

4 **Find the word that means something made of wood.**

dress ○   glove ○   brick ○   log ○

5 **Find the word that means something that makes honey.**

fish ○   bird ○   bee ○   cow ○

GO

Directions: Which answer means about the same as the underlined word?

SAMPLE B **choose them**
- ○ hear
- ○ help
- ○ see
- ○ pick

SAMPLE C **was awful**
- ○ bad
- ○ old
- ○ lazy
- ○ near

Directions: For numbers 6–11, choose the answer that means about the same as the underlined word.

6 nap now
- ○ race
- ○ sleep
- ○ stand
- ○ jump

7 be speedy
- ○ able
- ○ heavy
- ○ fast
- ○ better

8 beneath it
- ○ under
- ○ around
- ○ with
- ○ inside

9 will enjoy
- ○ miss
- ○ catch
- ○ like
- ○ dive

10 big rock
- ○ desk
- ○ stone
- ○ room
- ○ cliff

11 can wash
- ○ drink
- ○ float
- ○ hide
- ○ clean

GO

Directions: Which answer choice fits best in the blank?

SAMPLE
D   The _____ deer was shy. It stood beside its mother.

○ young   ○ brave

○ fast   ○ tall

TIPS   Try each answer in the blank.

Directions: For numbers 12–17, find the word that best fits in the blank.

12 **We must _____ soon or we will be late.**

○ play   ○ start

○ call   ○ study

13 **Put the ladder _____ the wall so I can climb up.**

○ inside   ○ along

○ against   ○ below

14 **Put the food on the _____ and then serve it.**

○ dishes   ○ floor

○ stove   ○ chairs

15 **The _____ was bright. It was easy to see even though it was night.**

○ moon   ○ cloud

○ sun   ○ fog

16 **Helena _____ her room blue and white.**

○ cleaned   ○ fixed

○ slept   ○ painted

17 **The cat's claws are _____ , so be careful when you play with it.**

○ soft   ○ sharp

○ furry   ○ nice

STOP

Lesson 3 Computation

Directions: Add to find the answer.

SAMPLE A

$$3 \\ + 2$$

- ○ 1
- ○ 5
- ○ 6
- ○ 32

Directions: Subtract to find the answer.

SAMPLE B

$$5 \\ - 1$$

- ○ 4
- ○ 6
- ○ 3
- ○ 15

1

$7 + 3 =$

- ○ 4
- ○ 21
- ○ 10
- ○ 37

2

$$4 \\ 1 \\ + 2$$

- ○ 7
- ○ 5
- ○ 3
- ○ 8

3

$10 + 30 =$

- ○ 20
- ○ 40
- ○ 13
- ○ 31

4

$$8 \\ - 2$$

- ○ 11
- ○ 6
- ○ 28
- ○ 10

5

$66¢ - 5¢ =$

- ○ 16¢
- ○ 61¢
- ○ 51¢
- ○ 65¢

6

$$14 \\ - 7$$

- ○ 21
- ○ 6
- ○ 7
- ○ 9

 Pay attention to the operation sign so you know what to do.

STOP

66

Lesson 4 | Review

Directions: Find the word that has the same beginning sound as <u>will</u>.

SAMPLE A

    saw   new   done   won

    ○   ○   ○   ○

1 **Find the word that has the same beginning sound as <u>four</u>.**

    corn   dark   fork   lift

    ○   ○   ○   ○

2 **Find the word that has the same beginning sound as <u>map</u>.**

    more   home   rest   smooth

    ○   ○   ○   ○

3 **Find the word that has the same beginning sound as <u>speak</u>.**

    dress   spill   slip

    ○   ○   ○

4 **Find the word that has the same ending sound as <u>leg</u>.**

    rug   gone   rich   grab

    ○   ○   ○   ○

5 **Find the word that has the same ending sound as <u>bread</u>.**

    dust   end   lose   sled

    ○   ○   ○   ○

6 **Find the word that has the same ending sound as <u>wild</u>.**

    hand   hold   toast

    ○   ○   ○

GO

Directions: Which word has the same middle sound as <u>bird</u>?

SAMPLE **B**

like	heard	noise	miss
○	○	○	○

7 **Find the word that has the same middle sound as <u>cow</u>.**

hope	roar	round	pop
○	○	○	○

8 **Find the word that has the same middle sound as <u>tent</u>.**

rest	team	seem	they
○	○	○	○

9 **Find the word that has the same middle sound as <u>rain</u>.**

load	that	bread	game
○	○	○	○

10 **Find the word that has the same middle sound as <u>fruit</u>.**

root	hope	boat	cow
○	○	○	○

11 **Find the word that has the same middle sound as <u>kite</u>.**

fair	list	have	five
○	○	○	○

12 **Find the word that has the same middle sound as <u>can</u>.**

bend	hand	what	don't
○	○	○	○

GO

Directions: Find the word that means something that you read.

SAMPLE
C

snack ○   book ○   seat ○   sound ○

---

13 **Which word means a small city?**

road ○   hill ○   house ○   town ○

---

14 **Which word means a body of water?**

lake ○   field ○   tree ○   cave ○

Directions: Find the word that means about the same as the underlined word.

15 <u>search</u> for

○ race
○ jump
○ look
○ write

16 large <u>boat</u>

○ wagon
○ balloon
○ cart
○ ship

17 will <u>listen</u>

○ hear
○ taste
○ find
○ sell

18 <u>wet</u> cloth

○ damp
○ small
○ soft
○ warm

GO

Directions: Which answer choice fits best in the blank?

Directions: Which answer solves the problem?

SAMPLE D

The ice was so _____ . We couldn't walk on it.

○ safe ○ thick

○ thin ○ cold

SAMPLE E

8
$+ 4$

○ 12
○ 4
○ 48
○ 84

---

19 The box was so heavy it took two of us to _____ it.

○ lift

○ see

○ find

20 The oven is hot. Now we can _____ the cookies.

○ taste

○ eat

○ buy

○ bake

21 Put your coat in the _____ and then close the door.

○ garden

○ box

○ closet

22

$11¢ + 61¢ =$

○ 50¢
○ 52¢
○ 72¢
○ 73¢

23

$9 + 9 =$

○ 99
○ 0
○ 19
○ 18

24

$44¢$
$- 24¢$

○ 68¢
○ 20¢
○ 60¢
○ 28¢

25

$62 - 4 =$

○ 52
○ 66
○ 12
○ 58

STOP

Mathematics

Lesson 1 | Mathematics Skills

Directions: Rudy has one dollar. He used it to buy a book. After he paid for the book, he got 3 pennies back.

SAMPLE A **Which book did he buy?**

$.93

$.97

$.87

$.77

○   ○   ○   ○

Listen carefully. Think about the question while you look at the answer choices.

Listen for key words and numbers.

As soon as you know which answer is right, mark it and get ready for the next item.

If you aren't sure which answer is correct, take your best guess.

GO

Tammy's mother wanted to serve fruit in addition to cookies and cake at a party. She asked each child to draw a picture of the fruit he or she liked best.

1   **How many children liked apples best?**

1	2	3	4
○	○	○	○

GO

2   **Which fruit got the most votes?**

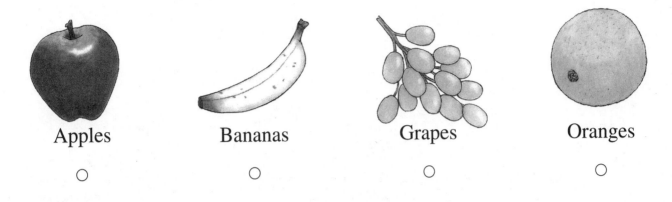

Apples   Bananas   Grapes   Oranges

○   ○   ○   ○

3   **Which fruit got two more votes than pears?**

Strawberries   Grapes   Apples   Bananas

○   ○   ○   ○

GO

4 **Which child is number 6 in line?**

○ ○ ○ ○

5 **Tommy's party started at 2:00. If the party lasted two and one-half hours, what time did the party end?**

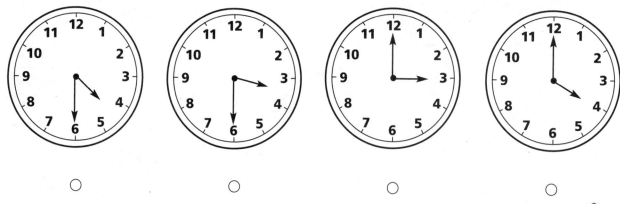

○ ○ ○ ○

GO

6

Directions: Find the round clock that tells the same time.

○   ○   ○   ○

Directions: Find the object that is as tall as 3 postage stamps.

7

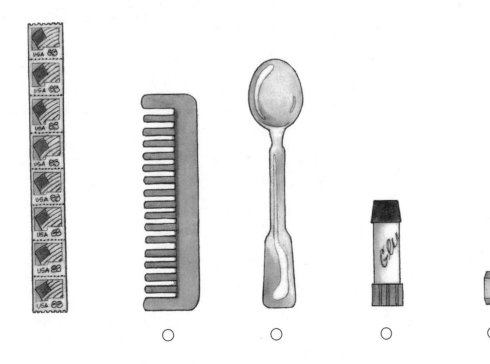

○   ○   ○   ○

STOP

Lesson 2 Review

Math Partners

Directions: How many blocks are in this tower?

SAMPLE A

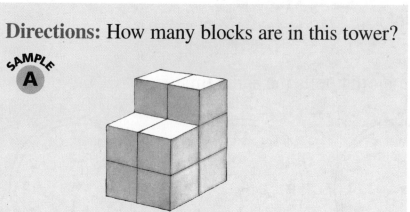

  6   8   10   12
  ○   ○   ○   ○

1 How many candies are there in all?

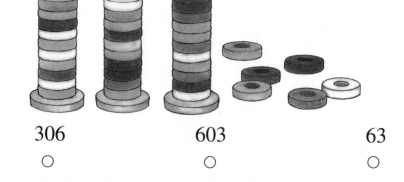

  36   306   603   63
  ○   ○   ○   ○

2 How much money is shown here?

  3¢   12¢   21¢   16¢
  ○   ○   ○   ○

GO

Directions: Look at the pattern in the box. Mark the answer that has the same kind of pattern.

3

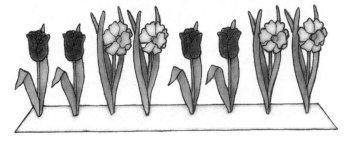

○

○

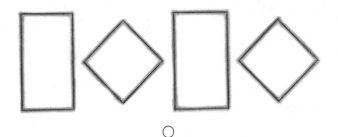

○

○

Directions: Find the picture that shows a group of 8.

4

GO

5 **Which number is 67?**

76   607   97   67

○   ○   ○   ○

6 **Ricky's father asked him to draw a triangle inside a circle.**

Which shape did Ricky draw?

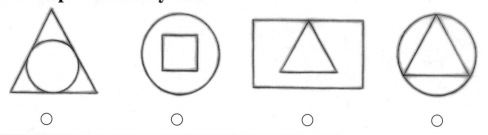

○   ○   ○   ○

7

9 stood on the edge of a lake.

4 went into the water.

How many ducks were left standing on the edge?

5   6   7   8
○   ○   ○   ○

8 **Ricky knocked down seven pins with his first ball.**

Which picture shows how many were left standing?

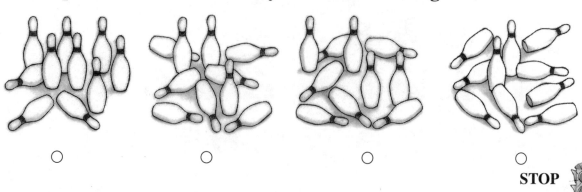

○   ○   ○   ○

STOP

0:40
Pages 79-84
Time Limit:
approx. 40 minutes

Final Test: Grade 1
Reading and Language Arts

UNIT 1

Reading and Language Arts

SAMPLE A

Flowers are pretty. They are also food for some animals like bees, other insects, and birds.

Who gets food from a flower?

a bee ○   a snake ○   a fish ○

Directions: Brenda is a butterfly who has a problem. Winter is coming and she is getting cold. Read the story about Brenda, then do numbers 1–5.

Brenda was cold. She had never been cold before. She lived in a sunny place that was usually warm. Brenda did not like being cold.

Brenda's friend, Ralph, saw that she was sad. "Why the long face?" asked Ralph.

"I'm cold," answered Brenda, "and I don't know what to do."

GO

Ralph grinned at Brenda. He answered, "My mother told me what to do. She said we should follow the other butterflies and fly south. It's warm there all the time."

Brenda and Ralph saw some other butterflies. They followed them south, and soon Brenda was happy again.

1 **Ralph says that Brenda has a "long face."**

He is saying that

○ Brenda's face is long.

○ Brenda looks sad.

○ Brenda is a very tall butterfly.

2 In the story,

Ralph grinned at Brenda.

What does this mean?

○ He was cold, too.

○ He didn't know what to do.

○ He smiled at her.

---

3 **Why was Brenda happy at the end of the story?**

○ She knows winter is coming.

○ She was warm again.

○ Ralph showed her how to fly.

---

4 **In which direction do Ralph and Brenda fly?**

○ north

○ west

○ south

5 **Birds sometimes go south for the winter. How else are they like butterflies?**

○ They both fly.

○ They both swim.

○ They both have six legs.

GO

Directions: For numbers 6 and 7, find the word that fits best in each blank in the story.

> While they were going south, Brenda and Ralph flew over a __(6)__ . They saw some __(7)__ in it and people swimming.

6 ○ field
   ○ lake
   ○ farm

7 ○ cars
   ○ trucks
   ○ boats

Directions: Find the word that can take the place of Brenda and Ralph.

8 Some children saw <u>Brenda and Ralph</u>.

   ○ them
   ○ they
   ○ it

Directions: Find the sentence that is written correctly.

9 ○ Many miles with their friends.
   ○ They flew to a warm place.
   ○ Tasty flowers all around.

STOP

Directions: Read the letter that one girl wrote to a friend. Then think about what you would say in a friendly letter. Write it on the lines below.

May 5, 2002

Dear Mia,
    I won my race at field day last week. I got a blue ribbon.
            Your friend,
            Liz

Directions: Think about what you would say in a friendly letter. Write it on the lines below.

_____

_____

_____

_____

_____

_____

GO

Directions: Read the story one child wrote.

Chick thought Duck was mad at him. Duck was sitting by himself. Chick asked Duck what was wrong. Chick gave him treats and toys. At last Duck explained. Duck was not mad. He just wanted to be alone for a while. He and Chick were still best friends.

Directions: Think about a story you would like to write. Fill in the story map.

Beginning

Middle

Ending

Directions: Use your story map to write your story.

_____

_____

_____

_____

_____

_____

STOP

0:25
Pages 85-88
Time Limit:
approx. 25 minutes

Basic Skills

Directions: Find the word that has the same beginning sound as joke.

SAMPLE A

pay ○   jump ○   mop ○   funny ○

---

1   **Which word has the same beginning sound as pork?**

dust ○   late ○   pool ○   clap ○

---

2   **Which word has the same beginning sound as van?**

toast ○   move ○   near ○   vote ○

---

3   **Which word has the same beginning sound as chest?**

choose ○   touch ○   song ○   these ○

---

4   **Which word has the same ending sound as knob?**

coat ○   lunch ○   dear ○   club ○

---

5   **Which word has the same ending sound as stew?**

net ○   wheel ○   now ○   give ○

---

6   **Which word has the same ending sound as third?**

hard ○   land ○   barn ○   dark ○

GO

Directions: Find the word that has the same middle sound as <u>corn</u>?

SAMPLE
B

	bone	rose	fort	loud
	○	○	○	○

7 **Which word has the same middle sound as <u>watch</u>?**

lock	lead	home	roast
○	○	○	○

8 **Which word has the same middle sound as <u>ring</u>?**

find	chair	rise	sink
○	○	○	○

9 **Which word has the same middle sound as <u>bump</u>?**

young	four	show	coast
○	○	○	○

10 **Which word has the same middle sound as <u>nine</u>?**

six	rain	wild	find
○	○	○	○

11 **Which word has the same middle sound as <u>fun</u>?**

guess	great	jump	proud
○	○	○	○

12 **Which word has the same middle sound as <u>pin</u>?**

since	fast	stuff	soft
○	○	○	○

GO

Directions: Find the word that means a small horse.

SAMPLE C

cow ○   kitten ○   chick ○   pony ○

13 **Find the word that means a color.**

chalk ○   paint ○   light ○   brown ○

14 **Find the word that means a tool.**

hammer ○   make ○   fix ○   wood ○

Directions: Find the answer that means about the same as the underlined word.

15 speak quietly

- ○ talk
- ○ play
- ○ study
- ○ walk

16 muddy car

- ○ fast
- ○ large
- ○ dirty
- ○ shiny

17 remain here

- ○ leave
- ○ play
- ○ eat
- ○ stay

18 assist them

- ○ call
- ○ help
- ○ join
- ○ like

GO

Directions: For Sample D and numbers 19–21, choose the word that fits best in the blank.

SAMPLE D Everybody left _____ me. I stayed and helped clean up.

○ and   ○ above
○ beside   ○ except

19 Each week, I try to save some money in my _____ .

○ pocket

○ wallet

○ bank

20 The _____ at the beach were pretty. I took some home.

○ shells

○ water

○ crowd

21 I _____ the table. This made the books fall off.

○ bumped

○ saw

○ drew

○ liked

Directions: For Sample E and numbers 22–25, solve the problems.

SAMPLE E

$$8 - 4$$

○ 12
○ 4
○ 48
○ 3

22

$$45¢ + 42¢$$

○ 96¢
○ 3¢
○ 87¢
○ 83¢

23

$$8 + 2$$

○ 10
○ 6
○ 11
○ 28

24

$$50 - 50$$

○ 10
○ 5
○ 0
○ 100

25

$$12 - 7 =$$

○ 4
○ 6
○ 19
○ 5

STOP

Mathematics

SAMPLE A **Directions:** Which flag can be folded on the dotted line so the parts match?

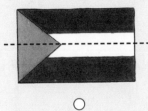 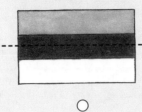 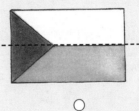 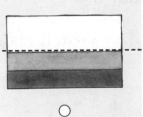

○   ○   ○   ○

1 **Which group has the largest number of nuts?**

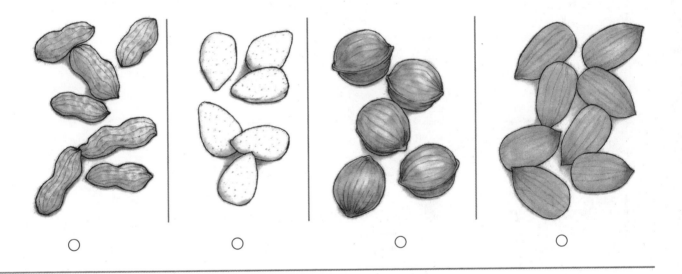

○   ○   ○   ○

2 **Which dress has both a triangle and a square on it?**

○   ○   ○   ○

GO

THE BOOK CLUB

Sam, Mindy, Paul, and Sasha are members of the book club. The graph shows how many books they read this week. Use the graph to answer numbers 3 and 4.

3 **Which child read the fewest books?**

Sam   Mindy   Paul   Sasha

○   ○   ○   ○

4 **Which children read the same number of books?**

Sam and Paul   Sam and Sasha   Sam and Mindy   Mindy and Sasha

○   ○   ○   ○

GO

5 **Which child is counting by fours?**

12, 13, 14   20, 24, 28   12, 18, 24   15, 18, 21

6 The pictures in the first row show how a piece of paper is folded and cut.
Find the shape that remains.

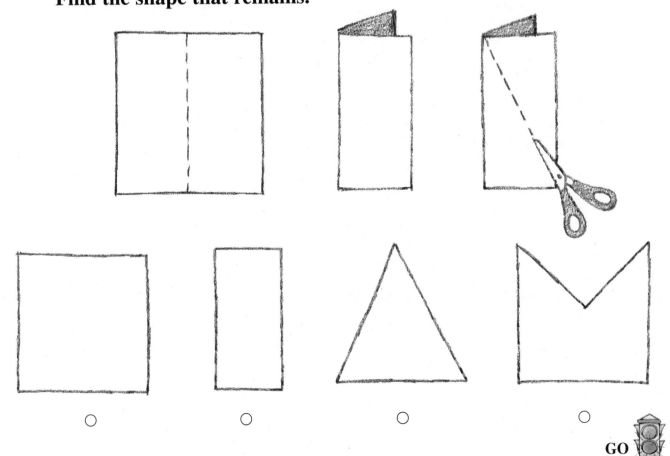

GO

Saving Our Money

Directions: The table has tally marks that show the coins that Sam, Mindy, Paul, and Sasha have. Use this table to answer numbers 7 and 8.

	Sam	Mindy	Paul	Sasha
penny	II	III	I	III
nickel	IIII	III	II	IIII
dime	III	I		
quarter		I	III	IIII

7 **Find the child who has the most coins.**

◯ ◯ ◯ ◯

8 **Find the child who has both a dime and a quarter.**

◯ ◯ ◯ ◯

STOP

Grade 2 Introduction to Practice Test and Final Test

The rest of this book is made up of two tests. On page 95, you will find Grade 2 Practice Test. On page 131, you will find Grade 2 Final Test. These tests will give you a chance to put the tips you have learned to work.

Here are some things to remember as you take these tests:

- Read and listen carefully to all the directions.

- Be sure you understand all the directions before you begin.

- Ask an adult questions about the directions if you do not understand them.

- Work as quickly as you can during each test.

- Using a pencil, make sure to fill in only one little answer circle for each question. Don't mark outside the circle. If you change an answer, be sure to erase your first mark completely.

- If you're not sure about an answer, you can guess.

- Use the tips you have learned whenever you can.

- It is OK to be a little nervous. You may even do better.

- When you complete all the lessons in this book, you will be on your way to test success!

Grade 2 Table of Contents

Practice Test

Unit 1: Reading and Language Arts

Lesson 1: Story Reading 95
Lesson 2: Reading a Poem 101
Lesson 3: Writing 105
Lesson 4: Review 107

Unit 2: Basic Skills

Lesson 1: Word Analysis 112
Lesson 2: Vocabulary 113
Lesson 3: Language Mechanics 115
Lesson 4: Spelling 117
Lesson 5: Computation 118
Lesson 6: Review 119

Unit 3: Mathematics

Lesson 1: Mathematics Skills 123
Lesson 2: Review 128

Final Test

Unit 1: Reading and Language Arts 131

Unit 2: Basic Skills 137

Unit 3: Mathematics 141

Answer Key 153

Reading and Language Arts

Lesson 1 **Story Reading**

SAMPLE A The wind was blowing hard and it was snowing. Because of the storm, school was closed. Pedro and Juanita could play outside.

in shorts
○

in a sweater
○

in warm clothes
○

SAMPLE B **Find the words that best complete the sentence.**

The _____ has lots of apples.

big tree
○

small bush
○

green lawn
○

Listen carefully to the directions.
Look at each answer before marking
the one you think is right.

New Things

Do you like to try things that are new and
different? Turn the page to read some
stories and a poem about new experiences.

GO

Directions: This is a story about a family looking for something.
Read the whole story and answer numbers 1–4.

The Surprise Kitten

Mrs. Jennings heard a noise.
She looked and looked around the house.
She couldn't find anything.

GO

Just then, Mr. Jennings came outside.
"Do you hear something?" asked Mrs. Jennings.
"Why, yes I do," answered Mr. Jennings.
Both of them looked and looked but still
couldn't find anything.

While they were looking, Jared came outside.
"What are you looking for?" he asked.
"We don't know," said his parents.
"How will you know if you find it?"
asked Jared.
Everyone laughed, then
Jared heard the sound.

GO

They were all searching in the bushes when Lettie stuck her head through an open window. "What are you doing?" she wondered out loud. "We are looking for something that is making a strange noise," said the three of them at once.

"Hmm," replied Lettie, "I think you are all in for a surprise. Look behind you." There on the lawn was a kitten. It said "meow" and walked up to the three of them. It wound its way among their legs and said "meow" again and again. Everyone laughed because they hadn't found the sound. It had found them.

GO

1   **Who said, "How will you know if you find it?"**

Mrs. Jennings
○

Jared
○

Lettie
○

2   **The kitten in this story**

○   is Jared's.

○   is sleepy.

○   is lost.

3   **Find the picture that shows where the Jennings family lives.**

○

○

○

GO

4 **Find the picture of what probably happened next.**

○

○

Directions: For numbers 5 and 6, find the sentence that fits best in the blank.

Directions: For numbers 7 and 8, find the word that can take the place of the underlined word or words.

5 **Mr. Jennings went shopping. He bought food for dinner.**

_____.

○ Then he came home.

○ Then he stayed at the store.

○ Then he sold the food.

6 **The kitten is hungry. Lettie knows what to do.**

_____.

○ The kitten runs away.

○ She gives it a bath.

○ She feeds the kitten.

7 Ned and I visited Jared.

○ He

○ We

○ They

8 Where is Lettie?

○ he

○ her

○ she

STOP

Lesson 2 Reading a Poem

SAMPLE A

A friend is someone you can trust
And ask a favor, if you must.

The writer thinks a friend is someone you can

play with.   depend on.   complain to.
○   ○   ○

Look back at the poem to find the answer.

Directions: Here is a poem about a child who flies in a plane for the first time. Read the poem and then do numbers 1–9.

Up and Away

I fasten my belt
And close my eyes;
The next time I look
We're up in the skies!

My very first chance
To soar like a bird
We're flying so high
I can't say a word.

Blue sky above;
White clouds below;
In a window seat
I enjoy the show.

Then the plane lands
And I head for the door.
I'm going to ask Mom
When I can fly more.

GO

1 **How is this child traveling?**

boat
○

car
○

plane
○

2 **What does the child do first?**

fix belt
○

eat food
○

read book
○

3 **What does the child see below?**

birds
○

clouds
○

stars
○

4 **Look at your answer for number 3. Where must the child be sitting?**

 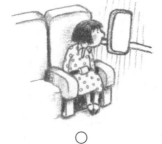 

○   ○   ○

GO

5   **If the child added a sentence to the poem about traveling with a relative, it might be**

> Beside me sat
> _____.

My best friend, Nat.
○

My sister, Pat.
○

A man with a hat.
○

---

6   **The child in the poem says**

> To soar like a bird.

To soar like a bird is to

step.
○

land.
○

fly.
○

---

7   **The child in the poem says**

> The next time I look
> We're up in the skies!

What does the child mean?

○   The plane rose quickly.

○   She saw the plane fly.

○   The plane is landing.

GO

8 In the poem, what is soaring?

train ○

plane ○

car ○

9 In this poem, the child <u>fastens</u> a belt. **What is the <u>opposite</u> of <u>fasten</u>?**

tighten ○

unfasten ○

attach ○

move ○

Directions: For numbers 10 and 11, find the sentence that best fits the blank.

10 People need clothes when they travel. _____. The suitcase is stored in the plane.

○ Planes are faster than cars.

○ An airport is a large building.

○ They put clothes in a suitcase.

11 An airport is a busy place. _____ . Planes take off and land all day.

○ You drive to get to the airport.

○ Many people come and go.

○ Sometimes a plane ride is long.

Directions: For numbers 12 and 13, choose the sentence that is written correctly.

12 ○ You need a ticket to fly in a plane.

○ Some people for a plane.

○ A seat belt for a bumpy plane ride.

13 ○ This is my seat.

○ Ticket in my pocket.

○ With my sister.

STOP

Lesson 3 Writing

Directions: Read the letter that one boy wrote to his grandmother.

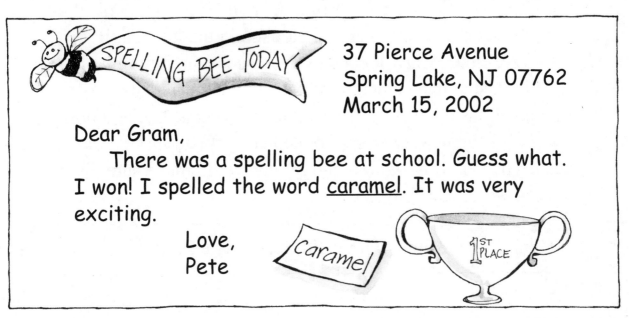

37 Pierce Avenue
Spring Lake, NJ 07762
March 15, 2002

Dear Gram,
    There was a spelling bee at school. Guess what.
I won! I spelled the word <u>caramel</u>. It was very
exciting.
            Love,
            Pete

Directions: Think about what you would say in a friendly letter. Write it on the lines below.

Directions: Read the story one child wrote.

One morning Chris couldn't find his homework. He looked in his folder. But it wasn't there. He looked in the kitchen. It wasn't there, either. Chris looked every place he could think of. Then he looked at his dog Ruff and had a hunch. Ruff liked to hide things in his dog bed. Chris's hunch was right. Under a dog pillow was his homework. Chris looked at Ruff and just shook his head. The next time, Chris thought, he would make sure his homework was in a safe place.

Directions: Think about a story you would like to write. Fill in the story map.

Beginning
Who?
When and where?
What is the problem?

Middle
What is the problem?

Ending
What is the problem?

Directions: Use your story map to write your story.

_____

_____

_____

STOP

Lesson 4 Review

SAMPLE A **Directions:** Mark the circle for the answer you think is correct.

Our neighbor is a gardener. One of her trees recently died. She said it was because of a bug.

From the story, you know that the neighbor's hobby is

gardening.
○

insects.
○

wood.
○

Directions: A new boy named Raj, who is deaf, came to Patsy's school. Raj was born in India, and he knows Sign Language, English, and Hindi, his family's language in India. This story is about Patsy's first experience with Raj. Read the story and then do numbers 1–7.

     **A New Friend**

"Can I sit here?" asked Raj in an unusual voice. He signed while he talked, and it was a little difficult to understand him.

"Sure," answered Patsy. She was very nervous, and her words barely came out. "What am I supposed to do?" she asked herself. "I've never met a deaf person before."

All that morning, Patsy kept looking over at Raj. He seemed to be able to understand what was going on in class. "How does he do that?" she wondered to herself.

That afternoon, Mrs. Martin took some time to let Raj and the other students get to know each other better. Patsy was surprised to find that her friend, Kyle, actually knew Sign Language. Soon, Patsy found she could understand most of what Raj was saying.

That afternoon, Raj and Patsy walked home together. Patsy learned some signs and told Raj about her family. By the time they reached Raj's house, she was able to sign "good-bye."

GO

1 Patsy said she was <u>nervous</u>.

Which of these words means the <u>opposite</u> of <u>nervous</u>?

calm   annoyed   frightened
○   ○   ○

---

2 Kyle <u>actually</u> knew Sign Language.

Which of these words means the same as <u>actually</u>?

rarely   really   seldom
○   ○   ○

---

3 **From the story, you know that Raj is**

embarrassed.   pleasant.   unfriendly.
○   ○   ○

---

4 **What did Patsy do at the end of the story?**

read a book   shake hands   sign "good-bye"
○   ○   ○

---

5 **In a few weeks, Patsy will probably**

○   forget Sign Language.

○   look for some other friends.

○   know more Sign Language.

GO

6   In the story, Raj has an <u>unusual</u> voice.

   Which of these words means the <u>opposite</u> of unusual?

   loud   regular   soft
   ○   ○   ○

---

7   **People would probably agree that Raj**

   ○   makes new friends easily.

   ○   has a hard time learning languages.

   ○   was more frightened than Patsy.

---

8   **Find the word that has the same vowel, or middle, sound as <u>found</u>.**

   road   flood   clown
   ○   ○   ○

---

9   **Which of these is the root, or base, word of <u>trying</u>?**

   try   ing   ryin
   ○   ○   ○

   * A base word is a word from
   which other words are made.

---

10   **Which of these is the root, or base, word of <u>reached</u>?**
   each   ched   reach
   ○   ○   ○

GO

11   **Choose the sentence that uses capital letters and end marks correctly.**

○   Raj was born in India.

○   he came to the United States last year.

○   His Family visits him often?

---

12   **Did <u>Leo and Elaine</u> finish the project?**

he
○

they
○

them
○

Directions: For numbers 13–15, find the answer choices with the correct capital letters and end marks for each missing part.

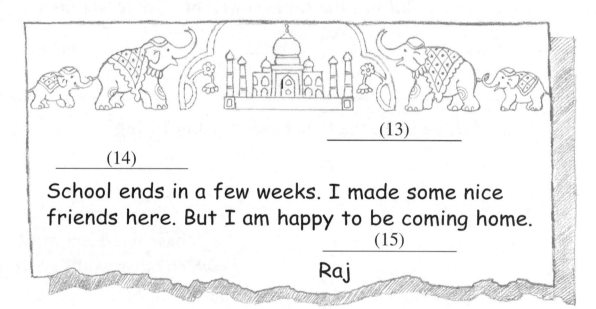

_____ (13)

_____(14)_____

School ends in a few weeks. I made some nice friends here. But I am happy to be coming home.

_____(15)_____

Raj

13   ○   May 5, 2001
        ○   May, 5, 2001
        ○   may 5, 2001

14   ○   Dear Mom
        ○   dear Mom,
        ○   Dear Mom,

15   ○   Your son,
        ○   your son
        ○   your Son,

STOP

Directions: Read the paragraph that describes an animal.

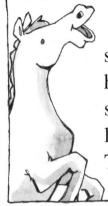

Horses are beautiful animals. Most horses have smooth, shiny coats and long manes and tails. Their hair may be brown, black, white, yellow, or even spotted. Sometimes horses neigh, or make a loud, long cry. Horses need to be brushed every day. This keeps them clean. Dirty horses may smell.

Directions: Think about an animal. Write words in the web that describe it.

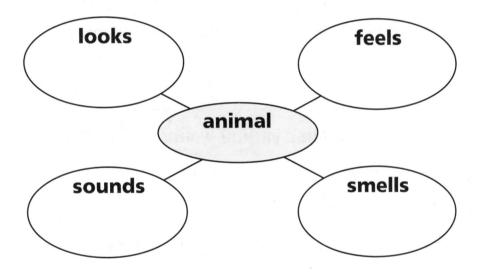

Directions: Write a paragraph that describes the animal.
Use the ideas in your web.

_____

_____

_____

_____

STOP

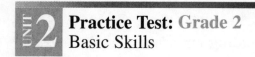
Basic Skills

Lesson 1 | Word Analysis

Directions: Find the word that has the same beginning sound as drink.

SAMPLE A
desk ○   dry ○   done ○

Listen to the directions while you look at the answer choices.

1 Which word has the same beginning sound as block?

box ○   breeze ○   blink ○

2 Which word has the same ending sound as build?

bell ○   cold ○   hard ○

3 Which word has the same vowel sound as rock?

hop ○   rode ○   stick ○   rake ○

4 Which word has the same vowel sound as join?

spoil ○   joke ○   grin ○   tool ○

5 Find the words that say what don't means.

did it ○   drive in ○   do think ○   do not ○

STOP

Lesson 2 Vocabulary

Directions: Which word means by yourself?

SAMPLE A
○ young   ○ alone
○ busy   ○ tired

Directions: Which answer means about the same as the underlined word?

SAMPLE B <u>large</u> room
○ pretty   ○ cold
○ big   ○ noisy

1 Which word means <u>choose</u>?

○ decide   ○ separate
○ sell   ○ fix

2 Find the word that means **lift up.**

○ find   ○ release
○ raise   ○ haul

3 Find the word that means **talk about.**

○ write   ○ enjoy
○ chase   ○ discuss

4 Find the word that means **bend toward.**

○ lean   ○ sleep
○ fall   ○ turn

Directions: For numbers 5–8, mark the circle for the answer that means about the same as the underlined word.

5 <u>muddy</u> clothes

○ loose   ○ baggy
○ cheap   ○ dirty

6 <u>normal</u> day

○ strange   ○ usual
○ long   ○ funny

7 full <u>bag</u>

○ sack   ○ can
○ barrel   ○ box

8 <u>hidden</u> place

○ open   ○ known
○ secret   ○ friendly

 Stay with your first answer.

GO

Directions: Which word fits best in the blank?

SAMPLE C   **The boat began to _____ .**

climb   wait   sink   talk
○   ○   ○   ○

Directions: For numbers 9 and 10, find the words that best complete the story.

The __(9)__ was easy to enter. All you had to do was show up at the park. To win, you had to __(10)__ how many jelly beans were in a jar.

9   ○   door   ○   tunnel   **10**   ○   play   ○   guess
      ○   contest   ○   room   ○   read   ○   count

Directions: For Sample D and numbers 11 and 12, which word fits best in both blanks?

SAMPLE D   **It was a _____ day. The speeder paid a _____ .**

nice   fine   ticket   great
○   ○   ○   ○

11   _____ the light over here.   **12**   The puppy began to _____ .
       The _____ on this pencil broke.   The car needs a new _____ .

       ○   point   ○   shine   ○   sleep   ○   light
       ○   eraser   ○   top   ○   run   ○   tire

Use the meaning of the sentence to find the answer.

STOP

114

Lesson 3 | Language Mechanics

Directions: For Sample A and number 1, decide which part needs a capital letter. If no capital letter is missing, choose "None."

SAMPLE A   Football practice ○ | will start ○ | on monday. ○ | None ○

1   when did ○ | you buy ○ | that bike? ○ | None ○

Directions: For Sample B and number 2, decide which punctuation mark is needed. If no punctuation mark is needed, write "None."

SAMPLE B   **This book is very funny**

? ○   . ○   None ○

2   **The phone is ringing**

. ○   ? ○   None ○

Directions: For Sample C and number 3, find the sentence that has correct capitalization and punctuation.

SAMPLE C
- ○ Pass this roll to randy.
- ○ Nothing is in the bag.
- ○ Dont' forget your coat.

3
- ○ Lennie isn't home
- ○ She is upstairs.
- ○ Who just called.

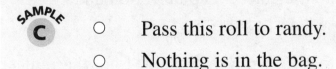

GO

Directions: Which answer choice fits best in the blank?

Directions: Which answer choice shows the correct capitalization and punctuation, or is it "Best as it is"?

SAMPLE D **Call _____ before you go.**

○ Jan miller

○ Jan Miller

○ jan Miller

SAMPLE E **The bus is <u>late today</u>.**

○ late Today

○ Late today

○ Best as it is

Directions: For numbers 4–6, choose the answer that fits best in the blank.

_____(5)_____

_____(4)_____

Thank you for the basketball. I have used it already. My friends like playing with it, too.

_____(6)_____

Sarah

4 ○ January 5, 2001

○ january 5, 2001

○ january 5 2001

5 ○ dear dad

○ Dear dad

○ Dear Dad,

6 ○ with love

○ With love,

○ with love,

Directions: Choose the answer that shows the correct capitalization and punctuation. If it's already correct, choose "Best as it is."

The window was <u>open When</u> it started to rain, I ran to close it. I got there just in time. The same thing happened when it rained <u>on Tuesday</u>.

7 ○ open when

○ open. When

○ Best as it is

8 ○ On Tuesday

○ on tuesday

○ Best as it is

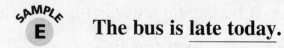

STOP

Lesson 4 Spelling

Directions: For Sample A and numbers 1–3, which word is spelled correctly and fits best in the blank?

Directions: For Sample B and numbers 4–6, find the word that is <u>not</u> spelled correctly. If all are spelled correctly, choose "All correct."

SAMPLE A

Did you_____ who was there?

- ○ notise
- ○ notisce
- ○ notice
- ○ notis

SAMPLE B

- ○ look <u>around</u>
- ○ <u>hidden</u> prize
- ○ never <u>mind</u>
- ○ All correct

1 Our _____ run is about two miles.

- ○ dailly
- ○ daley
- ○ dailey
- ○ daily

2 The _____ is open.

- ○ wendow
- ○ window
- ○ windo
- ○ windowe

3 The _____ is on the table.

- ○ butter
- ○ butterr
- ○ buter
- ○ budder

4

- ○ drop a <u>spoon</u>
- ○ fly a <u>plain</u>
- ○ <u>bunch</u> of flowers
- ○ All correct

5

- ○ <u>floating</u> log
- ○ <u>windy</u> day
- ○ <u>many</u> birds
- ○ All correct

6

- ○ hot <u>paivment</u>
- ○ strong <u>branch</u>
- ○ <u>right</u> answer
- ○ All correct

If an item is difficult, skip it and come back to it later.

STOP

Lesson 5 | Computation

Directions: For Sample A and numbers 1–3, solve the addition problems.

Directions: For Sample B and numbers 4–6, solve the subtraction or multiplication problems.

SAMPLE A

$$\begin{array}{r} 4 \\ + 6 \\ \hline \end{array}$$

○ 2
○ 10
○ 24
○ 46

SAMPLE B

$$\begin{array}{r} 8 \\ - 4 \\ \hline \end{array}$$

○ 4
○ 5
○ 12
○ 32

TIPS Pay attention to the operation sign so you know what to do.

1

$40 + 10 =$

○ 30
○ 40
○ 50
○ 60

4

$$\begin{array}{r} 7 \\ - 5 \\ \hline \end{array}$$

○ 15
○ 4
○ 12
○ 2

2

$$\begin{array}{r} 28¢ \\ + 23¢ \\ \hline \end{array}$$

○ 51¢
○ 55¢
○ 45¢
○ 50¢

5

$$\begin{array}{r} 44¢ \\ - 26¢ \\ \hline \end{array}$$

○ 22¢
○ 18¢
○ 28¢
○ 12¢

3

$38 + 9 =$

○ 31
○ 47
○ 49
○ 57

6

$$\begin{array}{r} 3 \\ \times 2 \\ \hline \end{array}$$

○ 1
○ 5
○ 6
○ 23

STOP

Lesson 6 Review

Directions: Find the word that has the same beginning sound as cry.

SAMPLE A

crush ○   climb ○   chew ○

Directions: Find the word that has the same vowel sound as home.

SAMPLE B

young ○   alone ○   busy ○   tired ○

1   **Which word has the same beginning sound as from?**

float ○   farm ○   fry ○

2   **Which word has the same vowel sound as read?**

round ○   rest ○   meet ○   late ○

3   **Look at the underlined word. Find the answer that tells what the contraction means.**

they're   they rest ○   they care ○   they run ○   they are ○

4   **Which word is a compound word?**

outside ○   repeat ○   follow ○   shopping ○

5   **Which word is a root word of faster?**

fas ○   fast ○   aster ○   ster ○

6   **Which answer choice is the suffix of rested?**

ted ○   rest ○   ed ○   sted ○

GO

Directions: Which word is something hot?

SAMPLE C
- ○ long
- ○ fire
- ○ poor
- ○ small

7 **Find the word that means something that flies.**
- ○ bird
- ○ fish
- ○ worm
- ○ dog

8 **Find the word that means part of a tree.**
- ○ shade
- ○ leaf
- ○ cool
- ○ moist

Directions: For Sample D and number 9, which answer means about the same as the underlined word?

SAMPLE D **hard riddle**
- ○ job
- ○ race
- ○ puzzle
- ○ portion

9 **to be certain**
- ○ late
- ○ worried
- ○ absent
- ○ sure

10 **Find the word that best completes both sentences.**

Hit the _____ with the hammer.
The _____ on my little finger is broken.
- ○ tack
- ○ skin
- ○ nail
- ○ wood

Directions: For numbers 11 and 12, find the words that best complete the story.

Each house on the block had a __(11)__ backyard. There were small patches of lawn, flowers, and even some __(12)__ gardens.

11
- ○ sloppy
- ○ neat
- ○ lost
- ○ loose

12
- ○ sand
- ○ recent
- ○ vegetable
- ○ unlikely

GO

Directions: For Sample E and number 13, which part of the sentence needs a capital letter? If no capital letter is missing, choose "None."

| SAMPLE E | The picnic ○ | took place ○ | last Saturday. ○ | None ○ |

13 | My friends ○ | will visit us ○ | on thanksgiving. ○ | None ○ |

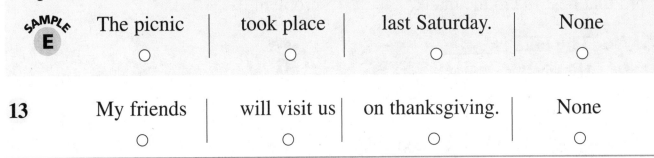

Monty Nelson
368 King Street

(14)

14   Choose the answer with correct capitalization and punctuation.

○ Wilson Pennsylvania 18302   ○ Wilson, Pennsylvania 18302

○ Wilson, pennsylvania 18302   ○ wilson, Pennsylvania 18302

Directions: For numbers 15 and 16, choose the answer that shows the correct capitalization and punctuation for each underlined part. If it's already correct, choose "Best as it is."

One holiday is special to our
(15) family. It is Labor day. We volunteer
at a local hospital so some of the
(16 workers can take the day off. It doesnt
bother us to work on this holiday.

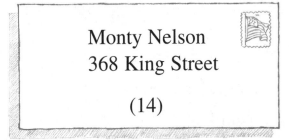

15 ○ labor day   **16** ○ doesn't

○ Labor Day   ○ does'nt

○ labor Day   ○ doesnt'

○ Best as it is   ○ Best as it is

GO

Directions: For Sample F and numbers 17 and 18, choose the correctly spelled word that best fits in the blank.

SAMPLE F **The lake is _____ that hill.**

○ beayond   ○ beyon

○ beyond   ○ beyont

17 **We _____ arrive around two o'clock.**

○ usully   ○ usuwally

○ usuelly   ○ usually

18 **A _____ blocked the sun.**

○ clowd   ○ cloud

○ clawd   ○ claud

Directions: For number 19 choose the underlined word that is not spelled correctly. If all the words in the group are spelled correctly, choose "All correct."

19 ○ nice <u>chare</u>

○ apple <u>tree</u>

○ <u>subtract</u> numbers

○ All correct

Directions: For Sample G and numbers 20–23, solve each problem.

SAMPLE G

$$\begin{array}{r} 6 \\ + 32 \\ \hline \end{array}$$

○ 38

○ 39

○ 56

○ 92

20

$415 + 25 =$

○ 390

○ 430

○ 440

○ 467

21

$$\begin{array}{r} 11 \\ 21 \\ + 32 \\ \hline \end{array}$$

○ 34

○ 53

○ 54

○ 64

22

$$\begin{array}{r} 54¢ \\ - 16¢ \\ \hline \end{array}$$

○ 42¢

○ 38¢

○ 60¢

○ 28¢

23

$3 × 5 =$

○ 31

○ 2

○ 8

○ 15

STOP

Mathematics

Lesson 1 | Mathematics Skills

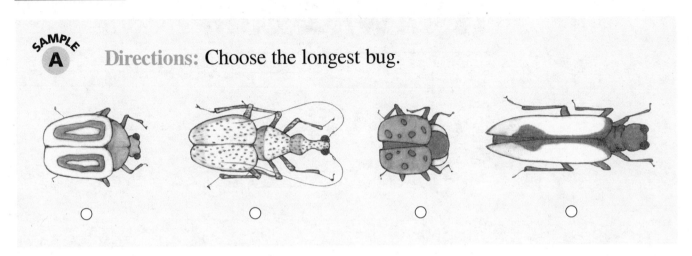

SAMPLE A **Directions:** Choose the longest bug.

○　　　○　　　○　　　○

 Listen carefully while you look at the problem and all the answer choices.

 Listen for key words and numbers.

 Mark the right answer as soon as you know which one it is. Then get ready for the next item.

GO

1 **What number is shown on the place value chart?**

36 ○   360 ○   306 ○   63 ○

---

2 **Find the shape that is one-third shaded.**

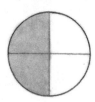   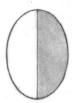   

Shape 1   Shape 2   Shape 3   Shape 4
○   ○   ○   ○

---

3 **Which number sentence can be used to show the total number of books?**

○ $4 + 2 = \square$ ○ $2 + 2 + 2 + 2 = \square$

○ $4 + 4 + 4 + 4 = \square$ ○ $4 + 4 = \square$

GO

4 **Which tool would students use to measure a pint of water from the stream?**

hanging scale	tape measure	measuring cup	thermometer
○	○	○	○

5 **Pablo has two quarters, one dime, and three nickels. How much money does he have in all?**

75¢	65¢	60¢	70¢
○	○	○	○

GO

6 **Which child is third from the lifeguard?**

Ann ○   Tom ○   Reg ○   Beth ○

---

7 **Which squares contain numbers that are all less than 19?**

○ 7 15 10 18   ○ 18 6 23 65

○ 91 20 32 57   ○ 12 81 17 44

---

8 **Which answer choice names a shape <u>not</u> in the circle?**

○ cone   ○ box
○ can   ○ ball

---

9 **Which number is missing from the pattern?**

3 5 7   11 13

6 ○   8 ○   9 ○   10 ○

GO

Directions: The students in Mr. Naldo's class are having a Math Fair. One of the games is a number wheel. The chart shows how many times the spinner landed on each number after 20 spins. Use the chart to do numbers 10 and 11.

10   **How many times did the spinner land on the number 3?**

   3   5   7   12
   ○   ○   ○   ○

11   **Which spinner looks most like the one the students are using?**

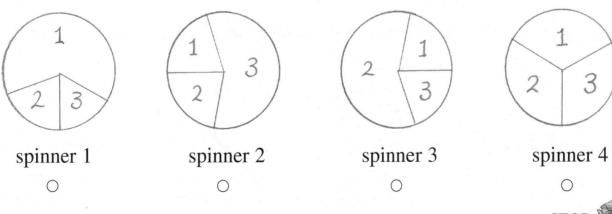

   spinner 1   spinner 2   spinner 3   spinner 4
   ○   ○   ○   ○

STOP

Lesson 2 Review

SAMPLE
A
Directions: A train left the station at 9:30. It arrived in Sharon Hill twenty minutes later. Which clock shows the time the train arrived?

○   ○   ○   ○

1 Four planes are on the ground at the airport. Two more planes land. How many planes are on the ground all together?

○ 8

○ 6

○ 7

○ 2

2 Find the calendar that has thirty-one days.

June	September	October	November

June   September   October   November
○   ○   ○   ○

GO

128

Directions: The bar graph shows how many fish are in a pond at a school's nature center. Use the graph to do numbers 3–5 on the next page.

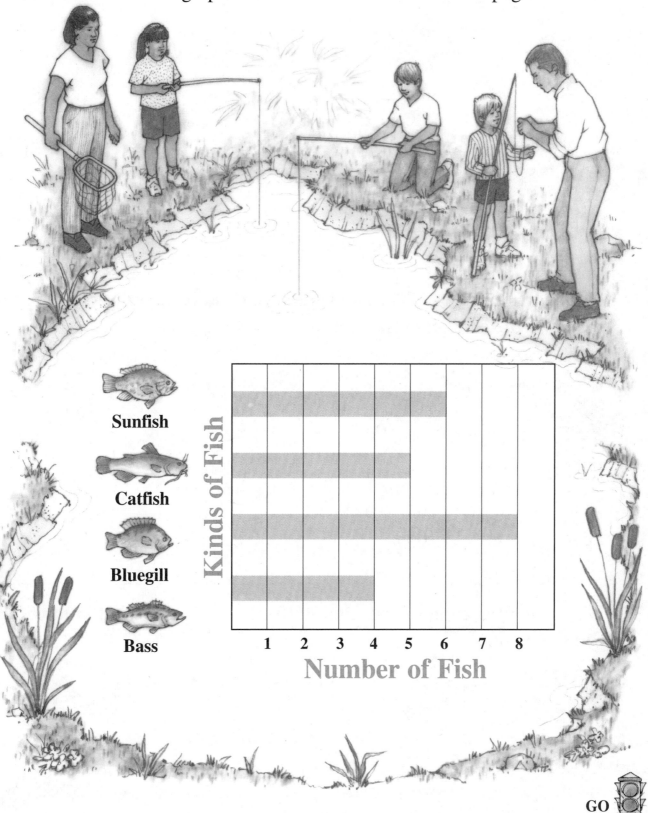

GO

3 **Look at the graph. What kind of fish are there fewest of in the pond?**

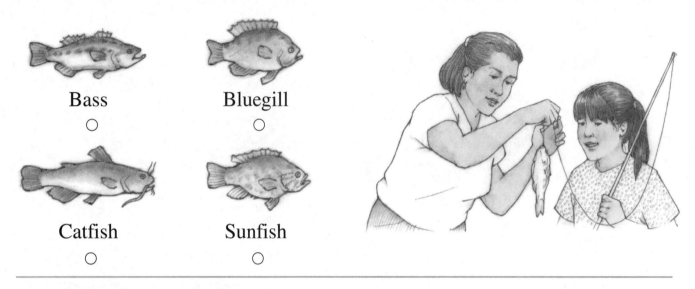

Bass
○

Bluegill
○

Catfish
○

Sunfish
○

4 **The average weight of the sunfish in the pond is six ounces. How much do the sunfish in the pond weigh all together?**

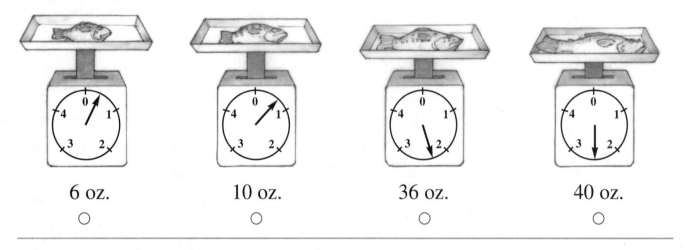

6 oz.
○

10 oz.
○

36 oz.
○

40 oz.
○

5 **Nadia counted eight of this kind of fish in the pond. What kind of fish did she count?**

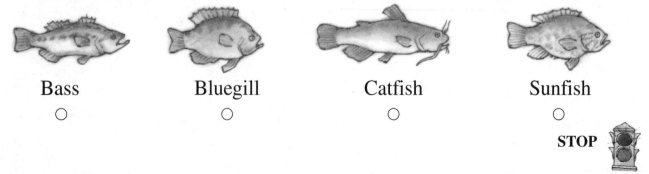

Bass
○

Bluegill
○

Catfish
○

Sunfish
○

STOP

Pages 131-136
Time Limit:
approx. 20 minutes

Final Test: Grade 2
Reading and Language Arts

UNIT 1

Reading and Language Arts

Directions: Read the story and answer the questions.

SAMPLE A

Jawan sat down at the table. He was hungry and the food looked awfully good.

What will Jawan do next?

go outside
○

read a book
○

eat dinner
○

Directions: This is a poem about something we take for granted. Read the poem and then do numbers 1–5.

WHY WHEELS?

Did you ever think
How it would feel
If nobody had
Invented the wheel?

Boats we'd have,
And rockets, too.
Sleds would work,
And a pair of shoes.

No bikes, no wagons,
No trucks or trains,
No cars to ride,
Not even planes.

But life would
Really be a bore,
If wonderful wheels
Were no more.

GO

Final Test: Grade 2
Reading and Language Arts

1 **What does it mean to <u>be a bore</u>?**

○   to be exciting

○   to be no fun

○   to be enjoyable

---

2 **Which of these does the writer not mention?**

○   sledding on snow

○   riding a horse

○   riding in cars

---

3 **Which of these is something that can fly but doesn't need wheels?**

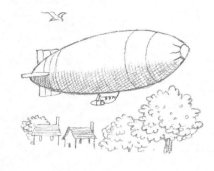

blimp   boat   bulldozer
○   ○   ○

---

4 **The writer of this poem thinks wheels are**

important.   useless.   unnecessary.
○   ○   ○

GO

5   **Why do planes need wheels?**

   ○   to land and take off

   ○   to fly high

   ○   to let people on and off

---

6   **Find the sentence that completes the story.**

My bike had a flat tire. _____ .
Then we went for a ride.

   ○   The bike is red and white.

   ○   I like to ride after school.

   ○   My sister and I fixed it.

7   **Which one of these is a compound word?**

   introduce   describe   overpass
      ○   ○   ○

8   **Find another compound word.**

   automatic   driveway   repeat
      ○   ○   ○

9   **Find another word with the same vowel, or middle,**
sound as <u>plane</u>.

   stain   than   stand
      ○   ○   ○

GO

Directions: Find the words that best complete the sentence.

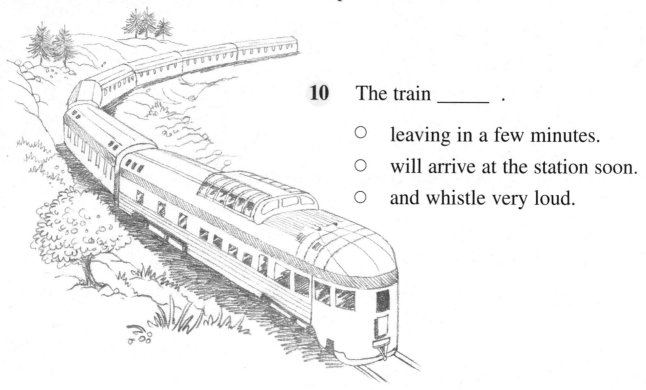

10   The train _____ .

  ○   leaving in a few minutes.

  ○   will arrive at the station soon.

  ○   and whistle very loud.

Directions: For numbers 11 and 12, find and then mark the part of the sentence that needs to be changed. If no part needs to be changed, mark "None."

11   My wagon | is in the garage | None
      ○   ○   ○

12   Did your brother | go with you? | None
      ○   ○   ○

STOP

134

Directions: Read the paragraph below that tells how to make a peanut butter sandwich.

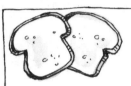

How to Make a Peanut Butter and Jelly Sandwich

You will need peanut butter and two pieces of bread. First, spread peanut butter on one piece of bread. Next, spread jelly on the other piece. Then, put the two pieces of bread together.
Last, cut the sandwich in half. Eat and enjoy!

Directions: Think of something you can do or make. Fill in the lines below to write a how-to paragraph.

How to _____

You will need _____

Steps:_____

_____

_____

_____

_____

_____

_____

GO

Directions: Read the paragraph that compares.

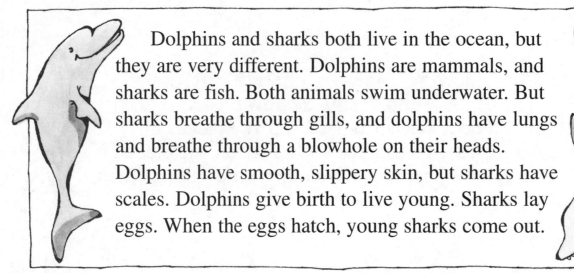

Dolphins and sharks both live in the ocean, but they are very different. Dolphins are mammals, and sharks are fish. Both animals swim underwater. But sharks breathe through gills, and dolphins have lungs and breathe through a blowhole on their heads. Dolphins have smooth, slippery skin, but sharks have scales. Dolphins give birth to live young. Sharks lay eggs. When the eggs hatch, young sharks come out.

Directions: Think of two animals or plants you know a lot about. Write a paragraph that compares them. Answer these questions:

- **What do they look like?**

- **Where do they live?**

- **How are they alike?**

- **How are they different?**

_____

_____

_____

_____

_____

_____

STOP

0:25
Pages 137-140
Time Limit:
approx. 25 minutes

Basic Skills

SAMPLE A **Directions:** Find the word that has the same ending sound as <u>camp</u>.

dump   trip   dirt
○   ○   ○

SAMPLE B **Directions:** Find the word that is a compound word, a word that is made up of two smaller words.

building   darkness   plumbing   sidewalk
○   ○   ○   ○

1 **Find the word that has the same ending sound as <u>best</u>.**

loss   salt   most
○   ○   ○

2 **Find the word that has the same vowel sound as <u>same</u>.**

ham   rain   soar   sand
○   ○   ○   ○

3 **What does the word <u>aren't</u> mean?**

are not   are late   are most   are then
○   ○   ○   ○

4 **Find the word that is a compound word.**

footprint   remember   narrow   explain
○   ○   ○   ○

5 **What is the root word of <u>kindness</u>?**

○
in   ness   kind   ind
○   ○   ○   ○

6 **What is suffix of <u>careful</u>?**

are   car   reful   ful
○   ○   ○   ○

GO

Directions: Which word means something that lights?

SAMPLE C
- ○ chair
- ○ door
- ○ hose
- ○ bulb

Directions: Which word means nearly the same as grateful?

SAMPLE D
- ○ thankful
- ○ busy
- ○ curious
- ○ finished

7 **Which word means to get better?**

- ○ trace
- ○ heal
- ○ sick
- ○ find

8 **Which word means a note?**

- ○ message
- ○ defeat
- ○ fashion
- ○ container

9 **Which answer means about the same as narrow?**

- ○ not busy
- ○ long
- ○ bumpy
- ○ not wide

10 **Find the word that best completes both sentences.**

Did you _____ your visitor well? My dog loves to get a _____ from me.

- ○ feed
- ○ snack
- ○ enjoy
- ○ treat

The line for the movie __(11)__ around the corner. This was a film that everyone wanted to see. Cindy __(12)__ there would be seats for them.

11
- ○ stood
- ○ arose
- ○ wound
- ○ lowered

12
- ○ hoped
- ○ called
- ○ bought
- ○ assisted

GO

Directions: In Sample E and number 13, decide which punctuation mark, if any, is needed in each sentence. If no punctuation is needed, choose "None."

SAMPLE E **Did you forget your hat**

. ○   ? ○   None ○

13 **This week it rained every day**

. ○   ? ○   None ○

Directions: For numbers 14 and 15, find the sentence that has the correct capitalization and punctuation.

14 ○ My birthday is in october.

○ Last Fall it was awfully warm.

○ In June we plant our garden.

15 ○ The bridge is high.

○ the road is new.

○ Where is the car

○ the keys are on the table

Directions: For numbers 16 and 17, choose the answer that shows the correct captalization and punctuation for each underlined part. If the underlined part is correct, choose "Best as it is."

(16)   We usually take our <u>vacation in July</u>. Mom and Dad rent a house at the beach.

(17)   <u>Its</u> not as big as our regular house, but everyone has a place to sleep.

16 ○ vacation in july

○ Vacation in July

○ Vacation in july

○ Best as it is

17 ○ It's not

○ it's not

○ Its' not

○ Best as it is

GO

Directions: For Sample F and numbers 18 and 19, choose the correctly spelled word.

SAMPLE F Be _____ near the pond.

- ○ carefull
- ○ cairful
- ○ carful
- ○ careful

18 Dad _____ some corn for dinner.

- ○ rosted
- ○ roasted
- ○ rowsted
- ○ roastd

19 Allan felt _____ in his new school.

- ○ lonley
- ○ loanly
- ○ lonely
- ○ loanley

Directions: For number 20 choose the underlined word that is <u>not</u> spelled correctly.

20
- ○ tasty <u>sandwhich</u>
- ○ huge <u>tiger</u>
- ○ <u>yellow</u> bird
- ○ All correct

Directions: For Sample G and numbers 21–24, solve the problem.

SAMPLE G

$$10 - 9$$

- ○ 0
- ○ 1
- ○ 19
- ○ 90

21

$$14 + 21 =$$

- ○ 62
- ○ 65
- ○ 36
- ○ 35

22

$$21 \\ 7 \\ + 6$$

- ○ 34
- ○ 24
- ○ 54
- ○ 44

23

$$874 \\ - 172$$

- ○ 1046
- ○ 802
- ○ 706
- ○ 702

24

$$2 \times 3 =$$

- ○ 1
- ○ 5
- ○ 6
- ○ 23

STOP

0:20
Pages 137-140
Time Limit:
approx. 20 minutes

Mathematics

Directions: If you are counting by ones, beginning with 42, find the empty box where 48 should be.

SAMPLE **A**

| 42 | 43 | 44 | | | | |

1. **How many inches long is the ear of corn? (from stalk to silk)**

○ 6 inches   ○ 5 inches   ○ 4 inches   ○ 3 inches

2. **Find the group of shapes that shows just one rectangle.**

Pair 1 ○

Pair 2 ○

Pair 3 ○

Pair 4 ○

3.

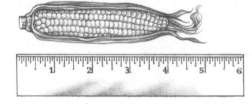

Rudy is hanging numbered keys on a board. Which numbered key should go in the box that is circled?

○ 77
○ 88
○ 89
○ 98

4 **Which coin can be removed from the second group so both groups have the same amount of money?**

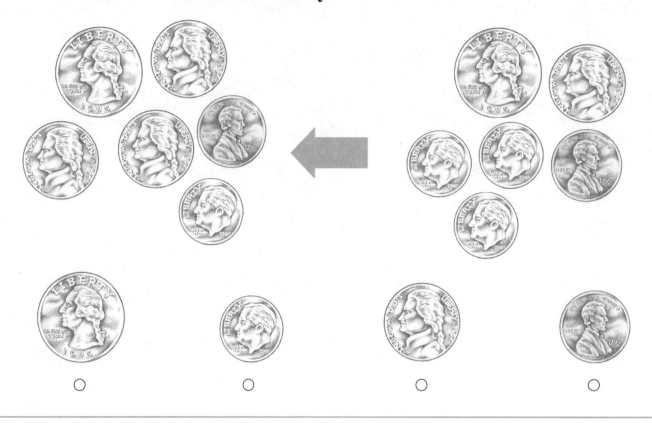

○   ○   ○   ○

---

5 **Find the fraction that tells what part of the set is circles.**

○ $\frac{5}{8}$

○ $\frac{3}{8}$

○ $\frac{3}{5}$

○ $\frac{1}{5}$

GO

6 Which number should the missing address be?

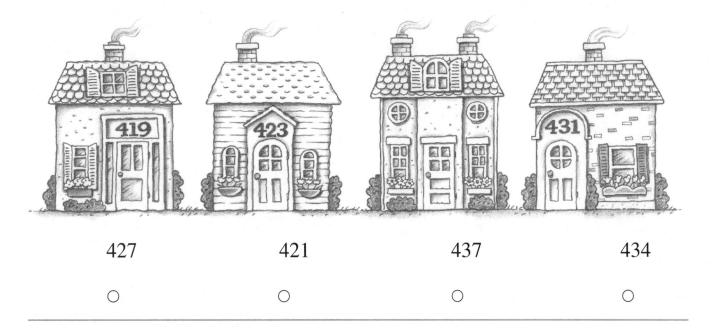

427   421   437   434

○   ○   ○   ○

7 Toshi made a shape on his geoboard. Paula wants to make the same shape. What will her geoboard look like?

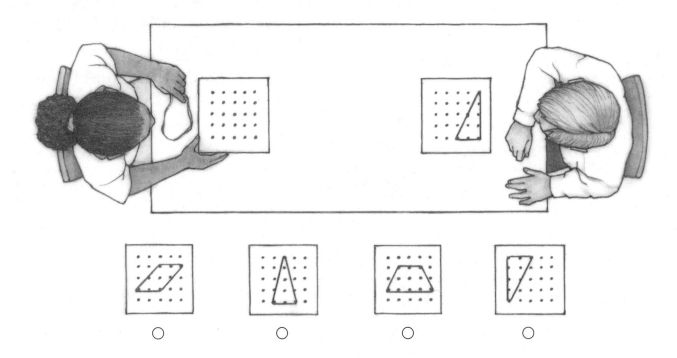

○   ○   ○   ○

GO

8 Elle saw that some t-shirts on a clothes line formed a pattern. If the pattern continued, which pair of the t-shirts would come next?

○   ○   ○   ○

9

Cliff counted 3 [hawk].

Georgia counted 9 [hawk].

Cliff counted 3 hawks on bird watch day. Georgia counted 9 hawks. Which number sentence could be used to find how many hawks they counted in all?

$9 - 3 = \square$ $3 + \square = 9$ $3 + 9 = \square$ $9 - \square = 3$

○   ○   ○   ○

STOP

144

Grade 1 Record Your Scores

After you have completed and checked each test, record your scores below. Do not count your answers for the sample questions or the writing pages.

Practice Test

Unit 1 Reading and Language Arts
Number of Questions: 37   Number Correct _____

Unit 2 Basic Skills
Number of Questions: 62   Number Correct _____

Unit 3 Mathematics
Number of Questions: 15   Number Correct _____

Final Test

Unit 1 Reading and Language Arts
Number of Questions: 9   Number Correct _____

Unit 2 Basic Skills
Number of Questions: 25   Number Correct _____

Unit 3 Mathematics
Number of Questions: 8   Number Correct _____

Grade 1 Answer Key

Page 26
1. tasty
2. under
3. rice
4. winner

Page 28
1. in the bowl
2. tall tree
3. drink water
4. party
5. careful

Page 30
1. den
2. rock
3. kind

Page 32
1. Sunday is the author's favorite day of the week, because she goes with her dad to play basketball in the park.
2. The author feels close to her father, because her father teaches her how to play basketball.
3. The book does not belong. The other two pictures show things you eat with.

Page 34
1. the second picture
2. Wendy wanted to eat cake.

Page 36
1. 40 cents
2. 14 books
3. 33
4. 64

Page 38
1. Bus
2. 15
3. Train

Page 40
1. Answers will vary but should tell what the child wants to learn to do, why, and how.

Page 43
A. on the dish
B. The owl was on the turtle.

Page 44
1. the third picture
2. the first picture
3. She was sad.
4. fixing a bike

Grade 1 Answer Key

Page 45
- **5.** strong
- **6.** fly
- **7.** line
- **8.** ten

Page 47
- **9.** He has long, brown hair.
- **10.** by the door
- **11.** bring it back.

Page 48
- **12.** My Dog Nick
- **13.** Is this Nick's ball?
- **14.** He

Page 49
- **15.** I wash the dog.
- **16.** Then I drink some milk.

Page 50
- **A.** kitten
- **B.** pick

Page 51
- **1.** the third picture
- **2.** the first picture
- **3.** the second picture

Page 52
- **4.** the first picture
- **5.** the third picture
- **6.** the second picture

Page 53
- **7.** leaf
- **8.** gone
- **9.** bag
- **10.** rest

Page 54
Answers will vary, but the child should answer questions about the animal chosen, such as how it looks, where it lives, what it eats, and some of the things it does.

Page 55
Answers will vary, but the child should write how-to sentences about something he or she can do or make using four steps.

Page 56
- **A.** eat
- **1.** foot
- **2.** second picture
- **3.** third picture

Grade 1 Answer Key

Page 57
  4. second picture
  5. second picture
  6. They were in the yard.
  7. what a bird did

Page 58
  8. comma
  9. period
  10. the coat
  11. chris

Page 59
Paragraphs will vary but should describe the child's special day.

Page 60
  A. boat
  1. neat
  2. desk
  3. from
  4. please
  5. skip

Page 61
  B. her
  6. can
  7. not
  8. love
  9. sent
  10. heart

Page 62
  C. must
  11. need
  12. cake
  13. sock
  14. eat

Page 63
  A. large
  1. year
  2. orange
  3. house
  4. log
  5. bee

Page 64
  B. pick
  C. bad
  6. sleep
  7. fast
  8. under
  9. like
  10. stone
  11. clean

Grade 1 Answer Key

Page 65
D. young
12. start
13. against
14. dishes
15. moon
16. painted
17. sharp

Page 66
A. 5
1. 10
2. 7
3. 40
B. 4
4. 6
5. 61 cents
6. 7

Page 67
A. won
1. fork
2. more
3. spill
4. rug
5. sled
6. hold

Page 68
B. heard
7. round
8. rest
9. game
10. root
11. five
12. hand

Page 69
C. book
13. town
14. lake
15. look
16. ship
17. hear
18. damp

Page 70
D. thin
19. lift
20. bake
21. closet
E. 12
22. 72 cents
23. 18
24. 20 cents
25. 58

Grade 1 Answer Key

Page 71
   A. second picture

Page 72
   1. 2

Page 73
   2. Grapes
   3. Bananas

Page 74
   4. the third circle
   5. the first picture

Page 75
   6. the third picture
   7. the glue

Page 76
   A. 10
   1. 36
   2. 16 cents

Page 77
   3. the second picture (ovals)
   4. the last picture

Page 78
   5. the last picture
   6. the last picture
   7. 5
   8. the second picture

Page 79
   A. a bee

Page 80
   1. Brenda looks sad.

Page 81
   2. He smiled at her.
   3. She was warm again.
   4. south
   5. They both fly.

Page 82
   6. lake
   7. boats
   8. them
   9. They flew to a warm place.

Page 83
Letters will vary, but the child should write a friendly letter.

Page 84
Stories will vary but should follow the story map.

Grade 1 Answer Key

Page 85
- **A.** jump
- **1.** pool
- **2.** vote
- **3.** choose
- **4.** club
- **5.** now
- **6.** hard

Page 86
- **B.** fort
- **7.** lock
- **8.** sink
- **9.** young
- **10.** find
- **11.** jump
- **12.** since

Page 87
- **C.** pony
- **13.** brown
- **14.** hammer
- **15.** talk
- **16.** dirty
- **17.** stay
- **18.** help

Page 88
- **D.** except
- **19.** bank
- **20.** shells
- **21.** bumped
- **E.** 4
- **22.** 87 cents
- **23.** 10
- **24.** 0
- **25.** 5

Page 89
- **A.** first picture
- **1.** last picture
- **2.** last picture

Page 90
- **3.** Paul
- **4.** Mindy and Sasha

Page 91
- **5.** second child
- **6.** third picture

Page 92
- **7.** last child
- **8.** second child

Grade 2 Record Your Scores

After you have completed and checked each test, record your scores below. Do not count your answers for the sample questions or the writing pages.

Practice Test

Unit 1 Reading and Language Arts
Number of Questions: 36   Number Correct _____

Unit 2 Basic Skills
Number of Questions: 60   Number Correct _____

Unit 3 Mathematics
Number of Questions: 16   Number Correct _____

Final Test

Unit 1 Reading and Language Arts
Number of Questions: 12   Number Correct _____

Unit 2 Basic Skills
Number of Questions: 24   Number Correct _____

Unit 3 Mathematics
Number of Questions: 9   Number Correct _____

Grade 2 Answer Key

Page 95
- **A.** in warm clothes
- **B.** big tree

Page 99
- **1.** Jared
- **2.** is lost.
- **3.** first picture

Page 100
- **4.** first picture
- **5.** Then he came home.
- **6.** She feeds the kitten.
- **7.** We
- **8.** she

Page 101
- **A.** depend on

Page 102
- **1.** plane
- **2.** fix belt
- **3.** clouds
- **4.** second picture

Page 103
- **5.** My sister, Pat
- **6.** fly
- **7.** The plane rose quickly.

Page 104
- **8.** plane
- **9.** unfasten
- **10.** They put clothes in a suitcase.
- **11.** Many people come and go.
- **12.** You need a ticket to fly in a plane.
- **13.** This is my seat.

Page 105
Child should write a friendly letter.

Page 106
Child should write a story using a story map.

Page 107
- **A.** gardening

Page 108
- **1.** calm
- **2.** really
- **3.** pleasant.
- **4.** sign "good-bye"
- **5.** know more Sign Language.

Grade 2 Answer Key

Page 109

6. regular

7. makes new friends easily.

8. clown

9. try

10. reach

Page 110

11. Raj was born in India.

12. they

13. May 5, 2001

14. Dear Mom,

15. Your son,

Page 111

The paragraph should describe an animal and use the ideas written in a web.

Page 112

A. dry

1. blink

2. cold

3. hop

4. spoil

5. do not

Page 113

A. alone

B. big

1. decide

2. raise

3. discuss

4. lean

5. dirty

6. usual

7. sack

8. secret

Page 114

C. sink

9. contest

10. guess

D. fine

11. point

12. tire

Page 115

A. on monday.

1. when did

B. period

2. period

C. Nothing is in the bag.

3. She is upstairs.

Grade 2 Answer Key

Page 116

D. Jan Miller

E. Best as it is

4. January 5, 2002

5. Dear Dad,

6. With love,

7. open. When

8. Best as it is

Page 117

A. notice

1. daily

2. window

3. butter

B. All correct

4. fly a plain

5. All correct

6. hot paivment

Page 118

A. 10

1. 50

2. 51 cents

3. 47

B. 4

4. 2

5. 18 cents

6. 6

Page 119

A. crush

B. alone

1. fry

2. meet

3. they are

4. outside

5. fast

6. ed

Page 120

C. fire

7. bird

8. leaf

D. puzzle

9. sure

10. nail

11. neat

12. vegetable

Page 121

E. None

13. on thanksgiving.

14. Wilson, Pennsylvania 18302

15. Labor Day

16. doesn't

Grade 2 Answer Key

Page 122
  F. beyond
  17. usually
  18. cloud
  19. nice chare
  G. 38
  20. 440
  21. 64
  22. 38 cents
  23. 15

Page 123
  A. last picture

Page 124
  1. 360
  2. Shape 4
  3. 2 + 2 + 2 + 2 =

Page 125
  4. measuring cup
  5. 75 cents

Page 126
  6. Beth
  7. 7 15 10 18
  8. box
  9. 9

Page 127
  10. 12
  11. spinner 2

Page 128
  A. third picture
  1. 6
  2. October

Page 130
  3. Bass
  4. 36 oz.
  5. Bluegill

Page 131
  A. eat dinner

Page 132
  1. to be no fun
  2. riding a horse
  3. blimp
  4. important

Page 133
  5. to land and take off
  6. My sister and I fixed it.
  7. overpass
  8. driveway
  9. stain

Grade 2 Answer Key

Page 134
  10. will arrive at the station soon.
  11. is in the garage
  12. None

Page 135
The child should write a how-to
paragraph telling what is needed and
what the steps are.

Page 136
The child should write a paragraph
that compares two animals or plants
he or she knows a lot about.

Page 137
  A. dump
  B. sidewalk
  1. most
  2. rain
  3. are not
  4. footprint
  5. kind
  6. ful

Page 138
  C. bulb
  7. heal
  8. message
  D. thankful
  9. not wide
  10. treat
  11. wound
  12. hoped

Page 139
  E. question mark
  13. period
  14. In June we plant our garden.
  15. The bridge is high.
  16. Best as it is
  17. It's not

Page 140
  F. Careful
  18. roasted
  19. lonely
  20. tasty sandwhich
  G. 1
  21. 35
  22. 34
  23. 702
  24. 6

Grade 2 Answer Key

Page 141

A. last box

1. 5 inches

2. Pair 4

3. 88

Page 142

4. second picture (dime)

5. 5/8

Page 143

6. 427

7. last picture

Page 144

8. first pair

9. 3 + 9 =

McGraw Hill Children's Publishing

All our workbooks meet school curriculum guidelines and correspond to The McGraw-Hill Companies classroom textbooks.

SPECTRUM SERIES

SPECTRUM WORKBOOKS FEATURING MERCER MAYER'S LITTLE CRITTER®
GRADES K–2

The nation's #1 educational publisher for grades K–12, together with the well-known Mercer Mayer's Little Critter® characters, represents a collaboration of two highly respected "institutions" in the fields of education and children's literature. Like other Spectrum titles, the length, breadth and depth of the activities in these workbooks enable children to learn a variety of skills about a single subject.

- Mercer Mayer's Little Critter family of characters has sold over 100 million books. These wholesome characters and stories appeal to both parents and teachers.

- These entertaining books are based on highly respected McGraw-Hill Companies' textbooks.

- Each book includes easy-to-follow instructions.

- Page counts range from 128–160 full-color pages.

NEW!
Spelling, Writing, and Language Arts for Grades K–2

- An answer key is included in each book.

TITLE	ISBN	PRICE
Gr. K - Math	1-57768-800-7	$8.95
Gr. 1 - Math	1-57768-801-5	$8.95
Gr. 2 - Math	1-57768-802-3	$8.95
Gr. K - Reading	1-57768-810-4	$8.95
Gr. 1 - Reading	1-57768-811-2	$8.95
Gr. 2 - Reading	1-57768-812-0	$8.95
Gr. K - Phonics	1-57768-820-1	$8.95
Gr. 1 - Phonics	1-57768-821-X	$8.95
Gr. 2 - Phonics	1-57768-822-8	$8.95
NEW Gr. K - Spelling	1-57768-830-9	$8.95
NEW Gr. 1 - Spelling	1-57768-831-7	$8.95
NEW Gr. 2 - Spelling	1-57768-832-5	$8.95
NEW Gr. K - Writing	1-57768-850-3	$8.95
NEW Gr. 1 - Writing	1-57768-851-1	$8.95
NEW Gr. 2 - Writing	1-57768-852-X	$8.95
NEW Gr. K - Language Arts	1-57768-840-6	$8.95
NEW Gr. 1 - Language Arts	1-57768-841-4	$8.95
NEW Gr. 2 - Language Arts	1-57768-842-2	$8.95

Prices subject to change without notice.

MATH
GRADES K–8

This series features easy-to-follow instructions that give students a clear path to success. This series includes comprehensive coverage of the basic skills, helping children master math fundamentals. Most titles have more than 150 full-color pages, including an answer key.

TITLE	ISBN	PRICE
Gr. K - Math *	1-57768-800-7	$8.95
Gr. 1 - Math *	1-57768-801-5	$8.95
Gr. 2 - Math *	1-57768-802-3	$8.95
Gr. 3 - Math	1-57768-403-6	$8.95
Gr. 4 - Math	1-57768-404-4	$8.95
Gr. 5 - Math	1-57768-405-2	$8.95
Gr. 6 - Math	1-57768-406-0	$8.95
Gr. 7 - Math	1-57768-407-9	$8.95
Gr. 8 - Math	1-57768-408-7	$8.95

* Illustrated by Mercer Mayer

READING
GRADES K–6

This full-color series creates an enjoyable reading environment, even for those who find reading challenging. Each book contains interesting content and colorful, compelling illustrations, so children are eager to find out what happens next. Most titles have more than 150 pages, including an answer key.

TITLE	ISBN	PRICE
Gr. K - Reading *	1-57768-810-4	$8.95
Gr. 1 - Reading *	1-57768-811-2	$8.95
Gr. 2 - Reading *	1-57768-812-0	$8.95
Gr. 3 - Reading	1-57768-463-X	$8.95
Gr. 4 - Reading	1-57768-464-8	$8.95
Gr. 5 - Reading	1-57768-465-6	$8.95
Gr. 6 - Reading	1-57768-466-4	$8.95

* Illustrated by Mercer Mayer

PHONICS/WORD STUDY
GRADES K–6

The books in this series provide everything children need to build multiple skills in language. Focusing on phonics, structural analysis, and dictionary skills, this series also offers creative ideas for using phonics and word study skills in language arts. Most titles have more than 200 pages, including an answer key.

TITLE	ISBN	PRICE
Gr. K - Phonics *	1-57768-820-1	$8.95
Gr. 1 - Phonics *	1-57768-821-X	$8.95
Gr. 2 - Phonics *	1-57768-822-8	$8.95
Gr. 3 - Phonics	1-57768-453-2	$8.95
Gr. 4 - Word Study & Phonics	1-57768-454-0	$8.95
Gr. 5 - Word Study & Phonics	1-57768-455-9	$8.95
Gr. 6 - Word Study & Phonics	1-57768-456-7	$8.95

* Illustrated by Mercer Mayer

SPELLING
GRADES K–6

This full-color series links spelling to reading and writing and increases skills in words and meanings, consonant and vowel spellings, and proofreading practice. Over 200 pages. Speller dictionary and answer key included.

TITLE	ISBN	PRICE
Gr. K - Spelling *	1-57768-830-9	$8.95
Gr. 1 - Spelling *	1-57768-831-7	$8.95
Gr. 2 - Spelling *	1-57768-832-5	$8.95
Gr. 3 - Spelling	1-57768-493-1	$8.95
Gr. 4 - Spelling	1-57768-494-X	$8.95
Gr. 5 - Spelling	1-57768-495-8	$8.95
Gr. 6 - Spelling	1-57768-496-6	$8.95

* Illustrated by Mercer Mayer

LANGUAGE ARTS
GRADES K–6

Encourages creativity and builds confidence by making writing fun! Seventy-two four-part lessons strengthen writing skills by focusing on parts of speech, word usage, sentence structure, punctuation, and proofreading. Each level includes a Writer's Handbook at the end of the book that offers writing tips. This series is based on the highly respected SRA/McGraw-Hill language arts series. More than 180 full-color pages.

TITLE	ISBN	PRICE
Gr. K - Language Arts *	1-57768-840-6	$8.95
Gr. 1 - Language Arts *	1-57768-841-4	$8.95
Gr. 2 - Language Arts *	1-57768-842-2	$8.95
Gr. 3 - Language Arts	1-57768-483-4	$8.95
Gr. 4 - Language Arts	1-57768-484-2	$8.95
Gr. 5 - Language Arts	1-57768-485-0	$8.95
Gr. 6 - Language Arts	1-57768-486-9	$8.95

* Illustrated by Mercer Mayer

WRITING
GRADES K–6

Lessons focus on creative and expository writing using clearly stated objectives and pre-writing exercises. Eight essential reading skills are applied. Activities include main idea, sequence, comparison, detail, fact and opinion, cause and effect, and making a point. Over 130 pages. Answer key included.

TITLE	ISBN	PRICE
Gr. K - Writing *	1-57768-850-3	$8.95
Gr. 1 - Writing *	1-57768-851-1	$8.95
Gr. 2 - Writing *	1-57768-852-X	$8.95
Gr. 3 - Writing	1-57768-913-5	$8.95
Gr. 4 - Writing	1-57768-914-3	$8.95
Gr. 5 - Writing	1-57768-915-1	$8.95
Gr. 6 - Writing	1-57768-916-X	$8.95

* Illustrated by Mercer Mayer

Prices subject to change without notice.